Books by

FICTION

Mystery
Death at Glacier Lake

Balky Point Adventures (MG/YA sci-fi)
The Universes Inside the Lighthouse
The Secret of the Dark Galaxy Stone

the Wishing Rock series (contemporary fiction) (novels with recipes)
Letters from Wishing Rock
The Wishing Rock Theory of Life
The Tides of Wishing Rock

NONFICTION

the Pam on the Map travel series (wit and wanderlust)
Pam on the Map: Iceland
Pam on the Map: Seattle Day Trips
Pam on the Map (Retrospective): Switzerland
Pam on the Map (Retrospective): Ireland

From the Wishing Rock Kitchens: Recipes from the Series

www.pamstucky.com
twitter.com/pamstucky
facebook.com/pamstuckyauthor
pinterest.com/pamstucky

Pam on the Map
SEATTLE
DAY TRIPS

Pam Stucky

This is more or less a work of nonfiction. Although the author and publisher have made every effort to ensure that the information in this book was correct at press time, the author and publisher do not assume and hereby disclaim any liability to any party for any loss, damage, or disruption caused by errors or omissions, whether such errors or omissions result from negligence, accident, or any other cause.

Copyright © 2017 Pam Stucky

All rights reserved. No part of this publication may be reproduced, distributed, or transmitted in any form or by any means, including photocopying, recording, or other electronic or mechanical methods, without the prior written permission of the publisher, except in the case of brief quotations embodied in critical reviews and certain other noncommercial uses permitted by copyright law. For information and permission requests contact www.pamstucky.com.

Published in the United States by Wishing Rock Press.

Cover photo © Pam Stucky
Cover design by Pam Stucky

ISBN: 1-940800-13-7 (print)
ISBN-13: 978-1-940800-13-4 (print)
eBook ISBN-13: 978-1-940800-14-1
eBook ISBN: 1-940800-14-5

www.wishingrockpress.com

for my trusty road trip sidekicks
Mom, Dad, Shannon, and Lisa
and all those who like to take the road less traveled

Contents

Introduction

As with most of the books I've written, I wrote *Pam on the Map: Seattle Day Trips* because it's the book I wanted to read.

I'm a Seattle-area native, born and raised. I love this area. Part of the appeal of the area is, of course, the fact that there's so much to do—not just in the city, but around the region.

What's more, I love a good day trip. I've often wished for a book that compiled some of the best day trips from the Seattle area. So when I couldn't find one I loved, I wrote one.

None of the Pam on the Map books are guidebooks, per se. However, if you've read other Pam on the Map books, or intend to read other Pam on the Map books (may I suggest *Pam on the Map: Iceland*?), you'll notice that *Seattle Day Trips* is much more practical and utilitarian; much more "guidebook-y." I even took the Pam on the Map tagline "Wit and Wanderlust" off the cover. The other Pam on the Map books are not just about the places I visited, but also about my experiences with and feelings about the destinations, and the people I met—from the mayor of Reykjavík to crime fiction authors to employees in a café or a visitor center.

Talking with the people who live in a place is one of the best ways to really immerse yourself in the place and get to know it.

In *Pam on the Map: Seattle Day Trips*, however, you'll find less chatting and interpreting, and more tips and ideas. Just the facts, ma'am! Well, mostly facts. Not completely. (I tell you this so you know what to expect of this book as well as the others in the series.)

I did personally take every trip in this book; many of them I've taken more than once. Unlike the other Pam on the Map books, that means that in this book I'm able to offer more insights and options than if I'd only had the one go at it.

And, as such, most of the itineraries are packed. Use them as suggestions and starting points, not as rules. Follow what you like; leave out what doesn't appeal to you. And if something along the way catches your interest that wasn't listed in the book, then by all means, always follow your curiosity. If you run out of time, you can always go again. Road trips are about discovery and the journey. On a road trip, the journey is the destination.

In general, my aim was to give you trips that take you around two or three hours away from Seattle. The Ruby Beach and Lake Quinault trip is the longest. At almost eight hours of driving alone, it does make for a very long day, but it's worth it.

If you like this book, be sure to go to my website and sign up for my mailing list (www.pamstucky.com). *Pam on the Map: Seattle Day Trips Book 2* is already in the works!

Pam Stucky

Using This Book

Distances:

Obviously the total distances listed in each trip are my own, based on my own starting point and my own meandering along the way. My starting point is in the north end; if your starting point is farther south, or anywhere else, adjust your expected distances accordingly.

Directions:

With a few exceptions, I have not included directions, but instead have included addresses (and/or in many cases, coordinates), since most of us are using our phones for directions, and roads change! In the Point Roberts chapter, I included more extensive directions as some people's cell phones might not work in the area.

Passes:

I've made my best effort to determine what passes are needed for parks and forests. However, there are so many different passes that it's well possible I've made an error. It's always a good idea to bring along some cash and a credit card in case you need to buy a day pass on the fly.

Optional Side Trips:

In each road trip, I've included a few optional side trips for those looking for further adventures. I've tried to include the information on each side trip more or less alongside the stops that are located nearby. In some cases, the side trip is geographically located before the first stop on the trip. In those instances, I've listed the side trip before the first stop, so you'll know in advance where it is, and not have to back track.

Photo Ops:

Let's face it: Western Washington and the Pacific Northwest are basically one continual photo opportunity. It would be impossible for me to list every great shot. However, on occasion there's a building, site, or view that I think is particularly noteworthy. In those cases, I've listed the photo ops along the route, and have attempted to give you an approximate location of where to find it.

Accuracy:

Things change. Always check conditions and opening hours before you go.

Maps:

I made the maps. I did my best. I'm not a cartographer. In some cases where all the points are very close together, I just put one or two general points. I advise you look at an actual map for more detail!

Disclaimer:

As with all Pam on the Map books, the opinions in this book are my own. While I always try to remain positive, kind, and considerate, my opinions and reviews can't be bought by any company, organization, individual, or other. I never will agree to give a positive review or account in exchange for a free anything.

The Day Trips:

Diablo Lake
Artist Point
Fairhaven and Bow–Edison
Point Roberts
Sequim
Ruby Beach and Lake Quinault
Westport
Mount Rainier / Paradise
Ellensburg, Cle Elum, and Roslyn
Leavenworth

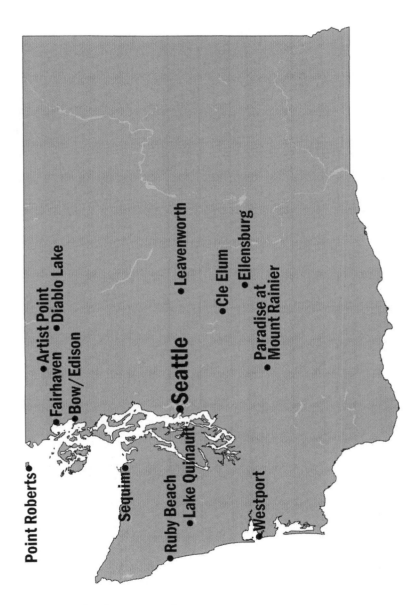

Map © Pam Stucky; not to scale

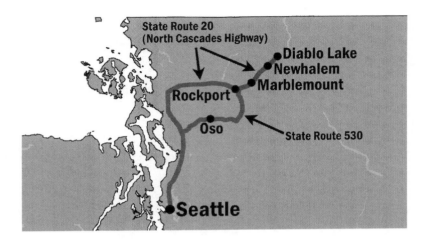

Stops:

1. Oso Landslide Memorial
2. Howard Miller Steelhead Park
3. Wildwood Chapel
4. Glacier Peak Winery
5. Marblemount
6. North Cascades Visitor Center
7. Skagit General Store in Newhalem
8. Ladder Creek Falls
9. Diablo Dam
10. North Cascades Environmental Learning Center
11. Diablo Lake Overlook
12. Rockport Pub

Diablo Lake

The North Cascades area has been called the "American Alps," and with good reason. This highway was the first National Scenic Highway in the U.S., and certainly remains among its most magnificent. Diablo Lake in the North Cascades mountain range, northeast of Seattle, is a man-made reservoir, created when Seattle City Light dammed the Skagit River in 1930.

Total miles driven: 265
Left home: 9:30 a.m.
Returned home: 4:30 p.m.

Diablo Lake is one of my favorite places, and this is one of my favorite Seattle day trips.

(Diablo Lake is the location of the cover photo of this book. Also, along with nearby Ross Lake Resort, Diablo Lake is the inspiration for the setting of my murder mystery, *Death at Glacier Lake.*)

The first time I ever visited Diablo Lake, it was summer, late

July. The rock flour was at its height (see more about rock flour below) and the lake was a breathtaking turquoise—literally breathtaking: I think I gasped when I first saw it. It's the kind of sight you want to stand and drink in with your eyes.

I've headed out to Diablo Lake more times than I can remember now, and I've never been disappointed. This year (2017) I even went in early March, driving all the way up to the Diablo Lake Overlook before being stopped by snow. The road to the overlook was clear, but the snow in the parking lot was about a foot deep. I and the other two carloads of people who had braved the conditions to get there parked on the side of the road outside the parking lot and walked carefully through the snow to the overlook railing. It was a sunny day, and the view down onto the lake was absolutely spectacular: the snow sparkling, the air crisp.

Of course, a mere week later an avalanche brought snow down over SR 20 at about milepost 123. The overlook is about nine miles beyond that, at about milepost 132, and the road was closed for the winter at milepost 134. Had I gone just before the avalanche, I would have been stuck between mileposts 123 and 134 for a couple of days. My point being: it's gorgeous in winter (and all year long), but be aware of conditions. Rock slides, avalanches, and other impassable events are not uncommon.

The North Cascades Highway is also part of the "Cascade Loop," which can't be traveled in a day (it's a huge and fabulous and scenic loop: see www.cascadeloop.com) but which nonetheless includes many spectacular points that are well worth a visit. Depending on the route you take on your trip, you may drive part of the "Mountain Loop Highway," which connects I-5 with SR 530 to loop through Arlington and Darrington, at which point the route diverges from this day trip and branches south and back to I-5.

Passes required:

No passes are required for any trailheads in the North Cascades National Park region. However, the US Forest Service does require a parking pass for some trailheads. Find a list of trailheads that require a parking pass here: www.fs.usda.gov/main/r6/passes-permits/recreation.

Important notes:

Roads: Due to avalanche risk, State Route (SR) 20, a.k.a. the "North Cascades Highway" is closed in winter from about milepost 134 (just past the Ross Dam Trailhead) to about milepost 178. Usually this is from sometime in November to sometime in April/May. For a look at historical open/closed dates, head to this site: www.wsdot.wa.gov/Traffic/Passes/NorthCascades/closurehistory.htm.

If you're heading out on this route and plan to go farther than Diablo, be sure to check the WSDOT website, www.wsdot.wa.gov/traffic/passes/northcascades/.

In the spring, especially if it's been a wet or snowy winter, avalanches or rock slides across SR 20 are not uncommon. It's never a bad idea to check road conditions on this route before you go.

Gas: The gas prices on your first stop on SR 530, at Arlington, exit 208, are surprisingly good. Nowadays, on trips north, I almost always gas up there. Out SR 20, your last chance to get gas on this trip is in Marblemount (unless you continue past Diablo all the way to Winthrop). Be sure to fill up there if you need to!

Food: You won't starve on this trip, but once you're off I-5 your food options diminish, and once you're past Marblemount, your only option is the tiny grocery at Newhalem … if it's not closed for the day or the season. This is a good trip for a cooler and a picnic! Be sure to bring water and anything else you might need.

Cell phone / internet: Once you're past Newhalem, your cell phone and internet connection will be sketchy at best, if not non-existent. Plan accordingly!

Getting there:

Heading north on I-5, you have two choices to get to Diablo Lake:
1.   Take I-5 to exit 208, SR 530 (Washington State Route 530), following SR 530 east past Arlington and Darrington, then north until it meets up with SR 20 and continuing east on SR 20 (this route includes the lower part of the "Mountain Loop Highway").
2.   Take I-5 to exit 230 and follow SR 20 the whole way out.

(You have the same options on the return, as well, so you could do one in one direction and another in the other.)

I've done both of the routes above, and generally I prefer to take SR 530. The routes take more or less the same amount of time, depending on traffic. SR 530 is prettier, and on hotter days feels a little cooler due to the trees lining much of the route. On the other hand, while it's usually open, it can occasionally be closed due to mudslides or roadwork, especially in summer, when they have to fill in the plentiful potholes that appear over winter. Construction delays can be long and wearying. Taking I-5 up to exit 230 feels faster, especially if 530 has delays, but is also less interesting visually.

If you take SR 530, note that you'll make a few jogs along the way. About 3.75 miles after you leave I-5, you'll need to jog left to follow SR 9 North for literally just about a tenth of a mile, before turning right again to get back on SR 530 East. In Darrington, at about milepost 49, the arterial road will come to a T. Take a left to stay on SR 530 (a right would take you south along the remainder of the Mountain Loop Highway).

If you take SR 20 the whole way, there are a couple of sections through small(ish) towns where you have to do some zigging and zagging on city streets, and the correct route might not be immediately obvious. Set your GPS and keep following signs to SR 20 East, and you'll get there!

Stops:

1. Oso Landslide Memorial
   (This memorial is along SR 530; so if you take I-5 to exit 230 and SR 20, rather than exit 208 and out SR 530, you won't see it.)
2. Howard Miller Steelhead Park
3. Wildwood Chapel
4. Glacier Peak Winery
5. Marblemount
6. North Cascades Visitor Center
7. Skagit General Store in Newhalem
8. Ladder Creek Falls
9. Diablo Dam
10. North Cascades Environmental Learning Center
11. Diablo Lake Overlook
12. Rockport Pub

As with many trips in this book, this is an out-and-back route (rather than a loop). Unlike many other road trips, when I go to Diablo

Lake I usually do all my stops on the way out, then drive straight home. Obviously, you can do them in whatever order you like.

Optional Side Trip:
Berries, berries, berries: If you take SR 530 rather than SR 20, you'll pass by Biringer Farm about two miles after you leave I-5. In berry season, you can U-pick strawberries and raspberries, or you can buy pre-picked berries by the flat, half flat, or basket.

Photo Ops:
SR 530 is a treasure trove of visual interest. From mountains and rivers and creeks, to rusty bridges and rickety fences, to barns and buildings in every stage of repair or disuse, to hand-lettered roadside signs advertising wood, fruit, and other goods, to a vintage closed gas station ... this route has it all. Be sure to bring your camera!

1. Oso Landslide Memorial

About four miles east of Oso, just past milepost 37
Map coordinates: 48.276419, -121.842534

On March 22, 2014, eighteen million tons of sand, clay, and till (enough to cover 600 football fields 10 feet deep) rumbled down the hillside about four miles east of Oso, Washington, killing forty-three people, destroying forty-nine homes and structures, and forever changing the landscape of hundreds of lives, as well as the earth itself. This 2014 Oso Landslide was the deadliest single landslide event in United States history.

As you approach milepost 37 (heading east on SR 530), you can see the remaining aftermath of the destruction on the left. In cleaning up the debris and clearing the road, the dirt and mud were herded into giant mounds which as yet have not been reclaimed by nature. The hillside from which the mud collapsed still stands with its open raw scar.

You can whip past this memorial without stopping; there's no notice that it's coming up, and you can easily be past it before you know you're upon it. Still, it's worth a stop. Take a moment to honor the people whose lives were lost, and to contemplate your own life, how everything can change in a moment. Maybe all those worries we have burdening us every day aren't as important as we think. The chance to live another day is something for which to be grateful.

2. Howard Miller Steelhead Park

52804 Rockport Park Rd
Rockport, WA 98283
(At the junction of SR 530 and SR 20)
Map coordinates: 48.484953, -121.595283
www.skagitcounty.net/hmsp

This wonderful little park is easy to miss, but don't miss it! It's located at the junction of SR 20 (about milepost 100) and SR 530 (northeast end of the road), so whichever route you take, you'll pass by it.

Coming from SR 530, Howard Miller Steelhead Park is immediately to the left after you cross the bridge that goes by Rockport, and just before SR 530 joins up with SR 20. The left turn into the park is almost hidden, and you might be tempted to take the second left that heads into the small town. Watch closely after the bridge for your turn.

Coming along SR 20, the park is at about milepost 100, off to the right in Rockport.

Although the crowning glory of Howard Miller Steelhead Park is not that it has restrooms, by this point in the trip that's always my reason for this first stop along the route. The restrooms are well maintained and are a welcome sight. Note that there's a Day Use area as well as a year-round camping area with available RV hook-ups. The restrooms on the camping side are for campers only. The Day Use area and restrooms are at the east end of the park.

While there, stop to look at the Tom Porter Cabin, where Tom Porter and his wife Mima (Kerr) raised six children. Tom was the seventh of ten children of Irish immigrants, born in Pennsylvania in 1852. He moved to this area sometime around 1880. Mima, also the child of Irish immigrants, was the twelfth of thirteen children, born in New Brunswick. She moved to the Marblemount area in 1889. They married on Christmas Eve of 1891. (See more about the Porters here: www.skagitriverjournal.com/Upriver/Sauk-Ill/Porter/Porter01-BioPhotos1.html.) The cabin itself is tiny, especially when you imagine six children in there. Most likely, though, they kids spent more time outside, and there's no question I would too. The Skagit River flows by this spot, with plenty of access points for you to walk down and dip your toes in. There's also a boat launch, if you happen to have brought a boat along.

Bald Eagle Bonus:
If you like bald eagles, you'll want to find out more about Howard Miller Steelhead Park. In winter, it's a (very cold) hot spot for bald eagle river tours. The Skagit River Bald Eagle Interpretive Center has its home at this park, and many river tours are launched from this area. Note, however, that the best viewing time is December to January or February, and it is very cold and almost certainly you'll

get wet. On the other hand, you might see upwards of fifty bald eagles on one trip, which is a sight to behold. Find out more about bald eagle viewing opportunities here skagiteagle.org/viewing-sites/ or search on your favorite search engine for Skagit River bald eagle tours or rafting tours.

Optional Side Trips:
Hiking in Howard Miller Steelhead Park: Several miles of walking trails can be accessed from the west end of the park (past the campsites).

Hiking in Rockport State Park: The town of Rockport and the Howard Miller Steelhead Park are on the south side of SR 20; Rockport State Park is on the north side. If you like a good hike, you might consider hopping across the street. The 670-acre park is home to an old growth forest that has never been logged; Douglas firs tower overhead up to 250 feet high. Hikers will find multitudes of options in the area. Leaving from the Rockport State Park parking lot, the Evergreen Trail is a three-mile trail that is fairly easy until the end, where it gets a bit steeper, though according to reports it is eroding in some places, so be careful. The Sauk Mountain trail is also just past Rockport, a very popular four-mile moderately difficult trail to the summit of Sauk Mountain with spectacular views. See more about Rockport State Park here: parks.state.wa.us/574/ Rockport.

3. Wildwood Chapel

58400-58698 N Cascades Hwy
Rockport, WA 98283
Map coordinates: 48.512235, -121.469107

Blink and you'll miss this tiny roadside chapel overlooking the
Skagit River. It's located just before Marblemount, at about milepost
103.9, on the east side of the road (on the right as you're heading
toward Diablo Lake). It's across the street from Clark Cabin Road
and Clark's Skagit River Resort (58468 Clark Cabin Rd, Rockport,
WA 98283). As you get close to the chapel, SR 20 curves to the left.
At the point where it curves, there are signs for Wildwood Chapel,
"500 feet ahead." There's a small turnaround by the chapel where
you can park while you go inside and sign the guest book. Pews on
either side will hold about a person and a half each, for a total of
six people and six half people. (That's just my estimate.)

Word has it the chapel is open at all times "for quiet reflection."
You can even reserve the chapel for very small weddings.

4. Glacier Peak Winery

58575 WA-20
Rockport, WA 98283
(360) 873-4073
www.glacierpeakwines.com

I've passed this winery so many times without stopping, so finally
on my winter visit earlier this year I peeked in just to see what
it was about. I was greeted by a very knowledgable hostess who
gave me the history of the winery while serving up nine wines (in-

cluding four dessert wines) for a tasting fee of $5.01. $5.01? Yes. $5.01. The sign says $5, but apparently there's a tax of some sort that makes it add up to $5.01. If you go, bring a penny (and $5).

Only a couple of the wines they offer for tasting are actually from grapes from their own vineyards; the rest are sourced from other eastern Washington locations. Are the wines any good? Here I'll acknowledge my own lack of wine expertise. My ratings for wine tend to be either "drinkable" or "not drinkable," with little distinction in between. I wasn't blown away by the wines, but what do I know? If you enjoy wineries and wine tastings, go and give them a try.

In winter, the winery is open for tastings Friday through Monday, noon to 6 p.m. In summer, starting June 1 and going through October, it's open seven days a week for those same hours.

5. Marblemount

Map coordinates: 48.526897, -121.434348

If you are low on gas, this is your last chance to gas up! (As of this writing, there are two gas stations there.)

Note that somewhere after Marblemount (I've never figured out exactly where), you're likely to lose internet connection.

I feel you should be warned here. Shortly after Marblemount, you're officially in the North Cascades National Park. The scenery here will take your breath away. This truly is one of the great scenic roads of the world. If you're driving, keep your eyes on the road! Believe me, I know it's hard sometimes! If it's been raining, tons of roadside waterfalls will be pouring down the mountain on your left, distracting you from the task at hand. Stay safe!

6. North Cascades Visitor Center

Just before "downtown" Newhalem on SR 20; around milepost 120
Map coordinates of entrance: 48.673472, -121.261460
www.nps.gov/noca/index.htm

Some might think visitor centers are boring, but that's actually rarely the case. Get the visitor center staff talking at pretty much any center around the world and you'll be regaled with tons of great information, whether specific to your needs or general to the area. For example, one of them might tell you that within the North Cascades National Park there are about three hundred glaciers, almost a hundred of them named—more than any other park in the lower forty-eight states.

This center is particularly well done and worth a visit. At the very least, it's worth a stop for their fantastic bulletin board area that lists hikes by length, difficulty, and accessibility, which can help you find the perfect trek for your own abilities. Some of the trails leave directly from the Visitor Center itself, including the short and very accessible Sterling Munro Trail (a 330-foot boardwalk trail with views of the Pickett Range) and the River Loop Trail (a loop trail just under two miles long, which winds through the forest to a gravel bar with river views). Check out the listings, or ask a staff member to help guide you on your way.

The exhibits at the center are also interesting and beautifully designed, and you have a chance to take a selfie with a (stuffed) bear or a giant banana slug; what more could you want?

This Visitor Center is not open in winter, so if you're on the seasonal cusp, check before you go to see whether it's open.

7. Skagit General Store in Newhalem

Slightly past milepost 120, North Cascades Highway 20
502 Newhalem St
Rockport, WA 98283
Map coordinates: 48.673197, -121.247012
(206) 386-4489
www.seattle.gov/light/damtours/store.asp

Winter hours Monday through Friday 9:30 a.m. To 4:40 p.m. Once the pass opens, hours extended, open 7 days a week

Newhalem is a tiny town (technically an "unincorporated community") built entirely for employees of Seattle City Light and the Skagit Hydroelectric Project dams. It's so remote that it seems amazing anyone would live there, but they do. And we're glad for it, considering how critical the hydroelectric power is to our region.

There's one primary road for visitors in Newhalem, aptly named Main Street, and the Skagit General Store is on it. (It's a one-way road, so go the right way!) The Skagit General Store is operated by Seattle City Light, and it's famous for its fudge. Head all the way to the end of the store to make your selection of cookies and cream, chocolate and praline, chocolate and walnut, or several other varieties.

If you're hoping to stop at the store, do be aware of hours. I've often gone by when it's been closed.

Directly across from the General Store is the Skagit Information Center. There's not much to it, but across the breezeway are clean and well-maintained restrooms. There are also water fountains with a built-in bottle filler, if you have your own bottle to refill. Pass through the breezeway to get a quick glimpse of the

"Temple of Power." (Note: some guides list the Temple of Power as a Marblemount attraction, but it is, in fact, in Newhalem.) Made from scraps of industrial electrical equipment, the Temple of Power is worth a glance if you're there.

Optional Side Trips:

Hiking: Several hiking trails, most of which are easy to moderate and accessible for most, leave from the Newhalem area, including the Trail of the Cedars (one-mile loop). The Trail of the Cedars is accessed by crossing a bridge just at the end of Main Street. It is fairly well maintained, with wide paths and just a few gentle slopes. Check the Information Center for more hiking options.

Newhalem Summer Softball Tournament: If you plan a trip the third weekend of July, check out the Newhalem Summer Softball Tournament, an annual event since 1977.

8. Ladder Creek Falls

Just past the main part of Newhalem
Map coordinates: 48.674482, -121.241517

Back on SR 20 East, continue a very short distance past the main part of the town. On the right, a giant building looms: the Gorge Powerhouse. This entire area is home to Seattle City Light workers and buildings. The Skagit River Hydroelectric Project, built from the 1920s through the early 50s, is a series of dams on the Skagit River built to provide hydroelectric power to the greater Seattle area. Almost ninety percent of the region's power comes from hydroelectric power; about twenty percent of Seattle City Light's electricity comes from the Skagit River system.

Turn down the short road to the right (before the powerhouse) and park. A suspension bridge beckons, and you must cross. It's a safe bridge, but it might be a little nerve-wracking for those who don't like heights. Also, it seems prone to bounce a bit if several people are walking on it at the same time. Behind the Gorge Powerhouse is a short and, dare I say, adorable trail alongside the Ladder Creek Falls. It's an uphill trek, steep at points with some steps, but not long at all, and worth the climb. Along the way you get beautiful views of the falls. There were a few points where you might expect to see fairies to come popping out of the magical, mossy landscape. It's a delightful trail, and one of my favorite finds on this trip. Again, be aware that this trail has many steps and might not be suitable for all people.

At night, the trail is illuminated with colored lights from dusk until midnight.

Optional Side Trips:
Powerhouse Insider Tour: In summer you can take the "Powerhouse Insider Tour," a three-hour guided tour through Newhalem and the Powerhouse itself. www.seattle.gov/light/damtours/skagittours.asp.

Dinner and Illuminated Falls: If you want to stay for the evening, and a dinner, a slideshow, and a walk through the illuminated Ladder Creek Falls Trail sounds like fun, check out the "Dam Good Chicken Dinner and Ladder Creek Falls by Night" tour: www.seattle.gov/light/damtours/night.asp.

These tours are not available year-round, so be sure to check the schedules.

9. North Cascades Environmental Learning Center / part of the North Cascades Institute

1940 Diablo Dam Rd
Diablo, WA 98283
(360) 854-2599
www.ncascades.org

Leaving the magical fairy woods of the Ladder Creek Falls behind, continue along the North Cascades Highway going east. At just about mile 127.5, a road branches off to the left: Diablo Dam Road. This leads down to the top of the dam, which is also a bridge/road that gives access to the North Cascades Environmental Learning Center.

This road is narrow and hugs the mountain in winding curves down to the lake, so be careful! When you got to the dam/bridge, complete with its picturesque lanterns that could be straight out of Narnia, you may wonder if it is okay to drive across it, as it looks more like a pedestrian bridge than a road. The answer is yes, you can drive across it. Keep your eyes open, though: the scenery is spectacular and there may well be people walking on the bridge and taking pictures. If you find yourself wondering whether there is room for two cars to pass each other in the middle of the bridge, the answer is also yes, but it's tight.

Diablo Dam is the second of three dams on the river. Upriver is the Ross Dam, and downriver is the Gorge Dam. If you are afraid of heights, hold on to someone while you look off the right-hand side down the full height of the Diablo Dam. Built between 1927 and 1930, the 389-foot-high Diablo Dam was for a short time the tallest dam in the world, until Oregon's Owyhee Dam came along two years later.

Depending on what time of year you're here, the lake on your right (Diablo Lake) will be anything from a basic, normal lake color to a breathtaking, startling milky glacial turquoise blue. I asked the North Cascades Institute about it, and a Program Manager at the Institute told me:

"The color of the lake and the amount of rock flour suspended in the lake is a seasonal thing. In the winter time, the alpine areas freeze up, so there is less movement of water and grinding of rocks by the glaciers. Most of the water coming into the lake in the winter is from rain. In the summer, we typically get less rain and it is the glaciers and snow melt that is providing the water coming into the lake."

Ever concerned for the environment, I also asked about climate change and its potential impact on the lakes. The Program Manager said:

"Climate change will have an effect on the glacial flour and color of the lake in the long term. Ross Lake is a totally different color because it is mainly snow and spring fed. Diablo Lake is mainly glacially fed, which is why it has that nice color in the summer. If the glaciers disappear in the high country, then they won't be there to grind down the rock and send that rock flour into the lake."

If you find yourself drawn by the beauty of the dam and the lake and needing to stop to admire it, after the dam/bridge there is a small parking area immediately around the turn to the right. Park, and hop out to explore the bridge and take in the views that defy superlatives.

Once you're done admiring this view, continue about half a mile down to the Learning Center. (Note: shortly after the turn, there are restrooms available in a small building on the left, with reasonably clean facilities. There are also clean facilities available at the Learning Center, at the end of the road.)

As you drive, on the right you'll see ferry parking. This is where visitors to the Ross Lake Resort park during their visit. The resort is accessible only by passenger ferry or by hiking in. See more about the resort in Optional Side Tours, below.

At the end of the road there's a gravel parking lot. Park and explore the nearby trails, and/or head to the Learning Center and talk to the wise and knowledgable staff.

Optional Side Trips:

Learning Center Activities: The sixteen-building Learning Center has a ton of activities available, from natural history and art excursions, to wilderness seminars, to author readings, to their annual Harvest Dinner, and more. Their space can also be booked for conferences and retreats. www.ncascades.org/signup.

Skagit Tours: Mentioned above for their "Powerhouse Insiders Tour" and "Dam Good Chicken Dinner and Ladder Creek Falls by Night" tour in Newhalem, from this site Skagit Tours offers a handful of afternoon cruises and lunch boat tours. www.ncascades.org/signup/programs/skagit-tours.

Tours are not available year-round, so be sure to check their schedules.

Ross Lake Resort: I'm going to tell you about a fabulous (I hear) resort, but before you get too excited, know this: the resort only takes reservations one year in advance, and all available openings are snapped up almost the second they're available. I'm writing this paragraph in March, and there is not one night at one cabin available for their entire June through October season. You can put yourself on a waiting list, as I have, but I've never had any luck. Not one day! Even with that understanding, you might want to check out the Ross Lake Resort. They offer equipment rental (boats, canoes, kayaks, fishing equipment) not just to people staying at their cabins, but also to campers and day visitors. It's not the cheapest, but it is secluded and it looks lovely! (As noted above, the quiet, isolated lake and resort inspired my first mystery, *Death at Glacier Lake*. It's fiction. As far as I know, there have not been murders at the resort.)

11. Diablo Lake Overlook (a.k.a. Diablo Lake Vista Point)

Milepost 132
Map coordinates: 48.709971, -121.096610

If you've seen pictures of Diablo Lake from above, chances are they were taken from this overlook. It is spectacular, and at any given time you're likely to find numerous people with giant cameras attempting to capture the glory. They will, of course, fail; there's nothing like seeing it in person.

Optional Side Trip:
Ross Lake Trailhead: This is about the last open spot in winter before the road closure. There's a short hike that takes you down to an area where you can see a waterfall; keep going and you get a bird's-eye view of the Ross Dam and the cabins of the Ross Lake Resort.

12. Rockport Pub

52807 Railroad Ave
Rockport, WA 98283
(360) 853-8664
www.facebook.com/margiesorenson333/

So I'm going to tell you a little story.

I've been out to Diablo Lake, and have gone past Rockport, more times than I can remember. Early on, I noticed the Rockport Pub, but was always busy on my way to get to the lake and never stopped.

When I started dreaming up this book, I thought, "I should go to that pub and see what it's like." I headed out on yet another trip to Diablo, and stopped at the pub. But when I got there, it looked a little unwelcoming from the outside. Feeling a little less than adventurous that day, and letting my introverted side take over, I chickened out.

On another, later trip, though, I decided to give it a try. As I often do when I'm alone at a restaurant, I sat myself down at a table and pulled out some writing, to give myself something to do. About a half dozen locals were at the bar, chatting and drinking happily.

I looked around, and there was no menu, and no one coming to offer me one; as far as I could tell there was just one person working in the back. As I was trying to figure out what to do next, a woman (customer) at the bar invited me to come up and sit with them. I did. We got to chatting and she asked me if I had met Margie, the owner. Margie came out and greeted me somewhat distractedly, like a person who is busy working and focused on what she's doing.

I asked if there was a menu. Margie said, "I'm making burgers, do you want one?" I said yes. And I'm telling you, that was one of the best burgers I'd had in a long time! Then Margie came out again and we chatted, and it turns out she is a wellspring of local history. She told me story after story, and I'm sure has dozens or hundreds more interesting stories just waiting to be told.

While I was there, another local came in to chat with Margie. It's clear this is a favorite gathering place that draws people from all around the area, and that Margie is a favorite as well.

I still don't know if there's an actual menu. "Hole in the wall" and "dive" could be words that apply here. But it's a hole in the wall well worth visiting, and just writing this I can't wait to go back! If you go, tell Margie I sent you.

After your burger (or whatever Margie is serving that day), your day is done. The return trip is the same route, backward, so if you wanted you could mix up these stops and do some on the way out and some on the way back.

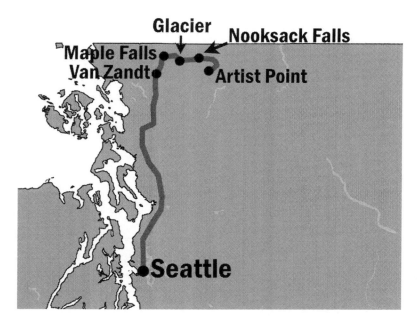

Stops:

1. The Everybody's Store
2. Mt. Baker Visitor Center
3. Picture Lake
4. Heather Meadows Visitor Center / Austin Pass Picnic Area
5. Artist Point
6. Nooksack Falls
7. Douglas Fir Campground
8. Graham's Store (attached to Graham's Restaurant)

Mount Baker / Artist Point

Mark your calendar to take this trip in August or September; at all other times of the year the snowpack prevents visitors from driving all the way to Artist Point, and you don't want to miss it!

Total miles driven: 280
Left home: 8:45 a.m.
Returned home: 6:15 p.m.

One fine Friday in April, I drove up to the Bellingham Visitor Center to see what suggestions they might have for a day trip in the area. I had the delightful luck of meeting Pat. Pat works at the Visitor Center on Friday mornings, but has lived in the area his entire life, he told me. I don't know how long that is, exactly, but I'd say it's a good handful of decades.

Pat gave me ideas for the Fairhaven and Bow–Edison Day Trip, and also suggested the stops on this trip. Seeing as he had such a wealth of wisdom from the area, I figured he knows what he's talking about! My instinct was correct. Artist Point is spectacular, and what's more, not nearly as crowded as Mount Rainier.

And The Everybody's Store is a stop not to be missed.

I recommend heading out to Artist Point early, after a quick stop at The Everybody's Store to pick up anything you need for a picnic. This will help you avoid any crowds. Also, in August and September, the trails can get very hot later in the day.

Passes required:

A Northwest Forest Pass or Interagency Annual Pass (America the Beautiful Pass) is needed for various parts of this trip. If you stop at the Douglas Fir Campground, you'll need to pay a $5 day use fee (cash), not covered by other passes.

Important notes:

Sunscreen: Artist Point is high altitude with no shade. Bring sunscreen!

Timing: As noted above, you can only drive out to Artist Point in August and September (approximately). The rest of the year you can drive part but not all of this route. If you go in other months, be sure to check ahead for road conditions and to see whether the sites you want to visit are open.

Gas: Your last chance to get gas before you're in the National Forest is at Maple Falls.

Canada: Maple Falls, WA, is only about 5 or 6 miles from the Canadian border, as the crow flies. Chances are your cell phone provider might think you're in Canada at some point and try to start charging you international roaming and data fees. Mine did. Keep an eye on your phone and turn it to airplane mode if needed.

Water: Bring plenty. It gets very hot and dry at the top of the mountain in the summer months.

Food: Whether you bring your own picnic or just might want to pick up some food along the way, it's not a bad idea to bring a cooler and ice packs.

Mountain driving: Does driving on roads with precipitous drop-offs make you nervous? If so, the last part of this route might pump up your adrenaline a bit. Even if it doesn't make you nervous, it might have that effect on others. You may encounter drivers who are driving over the center line. Be prepared!

Getting there:

Start by heading north on I-5. At the Burlington exit (Exit 230), head out State Route 20 to SR 9, and head north. (In Burlington you'll have to zig-zag a bit through town to stay on SR 20.)

Stops:

1. The Everybody's Store
2. Mt. Baker Visitor Center
3. Picture Lake
4. Heather Meadows Visitor Center / Austin Pass Picnic Area
5. Artist Point
6. Nooksack Falls
7. Douglas Fir Campground
8. Graham's Store (attached to Graham's Restaurant)

1. The Everybody's Store

5465 Potter Rd
Deming, WA 98244
(360) 592-2297
www.everybodys.com

"Stop first in Van Zandt," Pat told me. "There's a hippie's convenience store there. You've never seen anything like it. But you go in and there are great glass containers, this one with meat, that one with cheese ... it might be a good place to get food for your trip!"

This is how I find myself making my way to The Everybody's Store, and let me tell you, it is a wonder to behold. Not only is it a store for everybody, but it is a store with everything. When I stopped in, Jeff Margolis, the owner (along with his wife Amy) stopped what he was doing to give me a tour of both the store (as well as the town).

Sure, The Everybody's Store has your standards for this kind of place: firewood, water, toiletries, snacks, bug repellent, sunscreen, maps, and Recreation Passes for area activities. But that's just the beginning. You'll want to spend some time perusing the store because you will not believe what all you might find. Jeff and his wife, who have owned and run this store since 1970, like to seek out unique treasures you'd have to search far and wide for elsewhere. For example, at the time I stopped by, a clerk was just unpacking and getting ready for sale a shipment of nail files made from crystalized glass from the Czech Republic. Around the aisles I found a surprising number of xylophones. They have hats, clothes, lots of socks. Candy of every kind, ranging from the common to the artisan. Jams and jellies, all your food needs. Sunglasses. Prayer flags. Gloves. Incense. Maps. Guidebooks. A large selection of wines.

Their own locally ground coffee blend. Organic produce and frozen organic meats. Pickled eggs, vitamins, pasta, exotic teas, chicken feed, scarves, jewelry, necklaces, leggings, local ice cream from the nearby town of Acme, and so much more. You'll find it all here.

On your way out, don't forget the deli, that Pat mentioned! Pick up something for lunch from the vast array of organic choices. ("We are the oldest purveyor of organic and natural foods in Whatcom County," Jeff told me.) Ask for a taste of the Nokkelost, a traditional spiced Norwegian cheese, made from a thousand-year-old recipe, which the owners have made specially for the store. I had a taste in the morning, and had to stop by on my way back home to get more! (Seeing as I hand't brought a cooler, I needed to buy a small ready-to-use ice pack. Which, of course, they had.)

This store is a delight to visit and well worth a stop.

Note: The parking to the left of the store (as viewed looking at the front of the store) is for store patrons. Signs are posted for people seeking access to park across at the Community Center, but that's not you (unless you plan to do some river activities as well), so you're fine.

Also note: there is no public restroom at the store. There is a "honey bucket" outside, but I would not recommend it.

Optional Side Trip:
Downtown Van Zandt: Take a walk around the area and check out the community center, of which I could tell Jeff was very proud, and the park and play area behind it. "It was a real community effort to build," Jeff told me.

2. Mt. Baker Visitor Center

7509 Mt Baker Hwy
Maple Falls, WA 98266
(360) 599-1518
www.mtbakerchamber.org

Next on Pat's list: he told me to stop at Maple Falls, which he said is a "Bavarian town." He's right … in that it has a couple of Bavarian-themed buildings, but it's no Leavenworth.

This town is, however, the last place to get gas before you head into the forest, so stop if you need to. In addition, the people at the Mt. Baker Visitor Center are tremendously knowledgable and helpful. If you have questions about the route, or want tips on hikes to suit your level of experience and ability, stop in and have a chat!

You're within spitting distance of Canada now, so watch your phone. When I hit Maple Falls, Verizon texted me to welcome me to Canada and explain the data charges. I switched it to airplane mode very quickly!

At this point you're already on Highway 542, which you'll stay on for the rest of the trip out. If you need to turn off your data, you can go without GPS from this point and know as long as you stay on 542, you're on the right route.

3. Picture Lake

Map coordinates: 48.8666, -121.6779

Be sure to take your trip in August or September, or you'll miss Picnic Lake, the Heather Meadows Visitor Center, and Artist Point. Highway 542 is closed for "winter" for almost all of the year past the Mount Baker Ski Area. If, however, you've timed your trip right, continue on 542 out to Picture Lake. There are actually two lakes ("Mount Baker Lodge Lakes"); pass the first of the two (Highwood Lake) and follow the road to the right around the second lake. Here, the road becomes one-way, and parking is available on the left.

The Picture Lake trail is a very easy, ADA-accessible trail of slightly less than half a mile. As you walk the trail, it'll become easily apparent why it was named Picture Lake. Mount Shuksan dominates the view to the south-east of the lake, and in the right conditions (I imagine early morning) you can take one of those coveted mountain-mirrored-in-lake photographs.

At the intersection of the roads between the two lakes, be sure to check out the hexagonal basalt columns on the north side of the road (on the right just as the road became a one-way road). These spectacular rock formations were formed tens or hundreds of thousands of years ago as lava was cooling. The columns are abundant in this area (I've read that the smaller the column, the quicker the cooling was), so keep your eyes out for more!

If you're into geology, this area in general holds many treasures. Much of what you see of Mount Shuksan, for example, is made up of the Shuksan Greenschist, which geologists believe may have begun as rocks on the ocean floor more than 150 million years ago.

4. Heather Meadows Visitor Center / Austin Pass Picnic Area

Milepost 56 on Highway 542
www.fs.usda.gov/detail/mbs/about-forest/offices/?cid=
stelprdb5160279
Fee area: $5/vehicle/day; Recreation Passes are valid for this area

Next, make your way along Highway 542 to the Heather Meadows Visitor Center. (There's a vault toilet in the parking lot.) This area offers some great views and several hikes of various lengths and difficulties. Check out the scenery and head to the Visitor Center to talk with the on-duty ranger and find out more about what's available. You can also buy Recreation Passes here.

Be sure to apply sunscreen here if you haven't already! High altitude + no shade = sun burns!

Trails include:
Bagley Lakes Trail: .75-mile one way (1.5 miles round trip) trail along the eastern shore of Bagley Lake.
Fire and Ice Interpretive Trail: An easy .5-mile loop that's great for families and people of all abilities.

5. Artist Point

End of Highway 542
Map coordinates: 48.847054, -121.692604

Once you're here, you'll almost certainly vow to come again. The views from Artist Point are breathtaking, and even with moderate crowds, the scene is peaceful. It's the kind of place to come and refresh your soul.

To help you get your bearings: as you enter the parking lot, the road is heading directly south. Along the north side of the parking lot you'll find a placard showing the area and available trails. On the northeast end of the lot are toilets. Trails lead out in every direction from the parking lot. Pack your water and follow the trails that tempt you. Some are fairly level, but others can be steep and a little more troublesome, with occasional stairs. Regardless, you won't be at a loss for moments of awe and glorious views. If you packed a picnic, find a spot. Eat. Breathe. (And pack out your garbage!)

6. Nooksack Falls

Highway 542 between mileposts 40 and 41 (about 40.8)
Map coordinates 48.905486, -121.808620

"You have to walk in a ways, but it's worth it," Pat told me of Nooksack Falls. The truth is, you don't have to walk far at all, but it's definitely a much more potentially treacherous trek than others in this book. Exit Highway 542 onto Wells Creek Road (well marked in both directions) and travel about .6 miles on the one-lane gravel road to the parking lot (the road continues over the bridge after this). Park, and find the signage to the trail. Also note the many emphatic signs telling you how dangerous it is to climb over the fences and off the trails to try to get a better view of the falls. Heed them! You don't want to die today.

The trail itself is short but steep in places, and can barely be called a trail (unless I was on the wrong trail, in which case the trail is not well marked). Walk down to and along the fence to get your glimpse of these falls that drop 88 feet into the canyon below.

7. Douglas Fir Campground

Highway 542 between mileposts 35 and 36 (about 35.4)
Map coordinates 48.902250, -121.911887

This is more of an Optional Side Trip, but since it was on Pat's list and we know Pat knows his stuff, I'm including it here.

"At this campground you'll find enormous firs," Pat told me, "and also a raging river that maybe I shouldn't tell you about, because you won't want to leave." (I told him he had read my mind because I adore a good raging river.)

On my visit, I drove in to the picnic area looking for access to the raging river, but the only access I found was down a rather steep slope—more of a visitor-made trail than an actual trail people are intended to use. However, the river is indeed raging and beautiful. I suspect some of the actual campsites have better access to the river, but as many were busy I didn't have a chance to check them out.

There is a $5 day use fee for the picnic area, not covered by any other passes, so bring cash and be aware. If you find a public access area down to Pat's beloved river, let me know!

8. Graham's Store (attached to Graham's Restaurant)

9989 Mt Baker Hwy
Glacier, WA 98244
(360) 599-9883
www.facebook.com/Grahams-Restaurant-1532031637062878/

"Glacier has only two buildings," Pat explained. "One's a restaurant; the other is a large general store with the best ice cream in the county," Pat told me. As it turns out, Glacier does have a few more buildings than Pat indicated, but from what I can tell, Graham's Store (attached to Graham's Restaurant next door) is the general place he meant. They have maybe eight flavors of ice cream, and the chocolate peanut butter was delicious. Grab a treat for yourself before you head home.

As far as the return trip, you can head back to I-5 and head south, or go south on SR 9 for a bit, down to Sedro-Woolley or however far you like, to savor the peace and solitude of the backcountry!

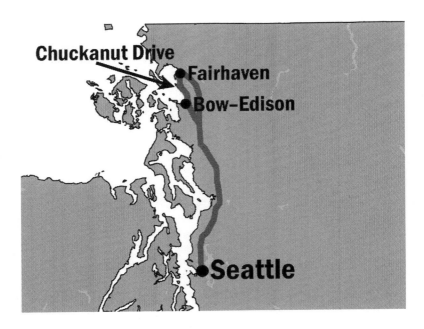

Stops:

1. Whatcom Falls Park
2. South Bay Trail and Woods Coffee
3. Downtown Fairhaven
4. Chuckanut Drive Scenic Byway
5. Chuckanut Manor and Sammy the Samish Bay Sea Monster
6. Downtown Edison
7. Samish Bay Cheese
8. Bow Hill Blueberries

Fairhaven and Bow-Edison

Historical meets nouveau hippie and farm fresh artisan in this trip to the scenic and agricultural north.

Total miles driven: 172
Left home: 9:00 a.m.
Returned home: 6:30 p.m.

Fairhaven is the historical district of the Bellingham area, a short drive south of the Western Washington University campus. The area was founded in the late 1880s, but within a few decades merged with two other pioneer towns into what is known today as Bellingham. The downtown core of Fairhaven, though, remains quaint, walkable, and full of great shops and spaces to visit.

According to fairhavenhistory.com, in 1977, Fairhaven was designated a historic district on the National Register of Historic Places with fourteen buildings of primary historical significance and three buildings of secondary significance. Today it is a great place for shopping, browsing, people watching, and dining.

The tiny town of Edison (often lumped together with nearby tiny town of Bow to be called Bow-Edison) is the kind of place where, upon visiting, people either start planning how they might move there, or they can't get away fast enough. As Christy, owner of Hedgerow told me, they either love it or "they don't get it." The area draws artists, foodies, and people wanting to live slow.

If you're looking for a day of traveling slow, meandering through shops, eating artisan food, browsing galleries filled with creations by local artists, making a connection with creators of both art and food, and then filling up your pantry and freezer with foods that you buy directly from the farmers, at their farms, this trip might be for you.

Passes required:

None.

Important notes:

Timing: While most of the stops I've included in the Bow-Edison area are open daily, to get the most bang for your buck you'll want to do this part of the trip on a Friday, Saturday, or Sunday, in the hours between 11 and 5. Many of Edison's few shops are closed the rest of the week.

This trip includes a lot of stops. Depending on how much you like to meander (and shop), you might want to split this into two trips: Bellingham/Fairhaven, and Bow-Edison.

Food: Pack a cooler and ice packs in case you want to pick up produce or meats in the various shops, or at roadside produce stands.

Getting there:

Head north on I-5. While I prefer driving Chuckanut Drive south to north, in this particular day trip I've included that part of the route north to south.

Stops:

1. Whatcom Falls Park
2. South Bay Trail and Woods Coffee
3. Downtown Fairhaven
4. Chuckanut Drive Scenic Byway
5. Chuckanut Manor and Sammy the Samish Bay Sea Monster
6. Downtown Edison
7. Samish Bay Cheese
8. Bow Hill Blueberries

1. Whatcom Falls Park

1401 Electric Ave
Bellingham, WA 98229
www.cob.org/services/recreation/parks-trails/Pages/whatcom-falls-park.aspx

Whatcom Falls Park is a delightful 241-acre multipurpose community park complete with picnic areas, a fish hatchery, basketball and tennis courts, forests, pools, about three and a half miles of trails, and, of course, the pièce de résistance, Whatcom Falls.

The easiest way to get to the actual falls is to park in the second parking lot at the end of Silver Beach Road (map coordinates 48.750968, -122.429028). (If you input into your GPS the official park address, 1401 Electric Ave, when you get inside the park entrance, turn off of Electric Ave onto Sunset St, and then instead of veering right onto Sunset Ln, turn left onto Arbor Ct. Follow this to Silver Beach Rd, where you'll turn right. Follow this a short distance to the parking lot.)

The access point for the trail to the falls is toward the middle/top of the north/west side of the parking lot. Look for a trail marked "To Falls." (Follow you ears, too; you can hear the falls from here.) The trail is easy and quite short, and takes you to a beautiful stone bridge overlook of the falls. The bridge, by the way, was a WPA project in 1939.

Optional Side Trips:

Interactive fun: For a mere $3 you can gain entrance to Mindport (210 West Holly St, Bellingham, WA 98225). Billing itself as "an inspiring blend of fine art and hand-built interactive exhibits to spark your awareness and stimulate your thinking," Mindport is a fun and inexpensive adventure. Be sure to check out the "Backwards Speech" exhibit, as well as "Allella," a mesmerizing music player exhibit.

Bioluminescence Paddle Trip: Not a day trip, but an interesting adventure nonetheless. During summer, the local Community Boating Center offers late night "Bioluminescence Paddle" opportunities, in which kayakers have a chance to experience the magical bioluminescence that occurs when certain plankton (only present in summer) are disturbed and light up. www.boatingcenter.org/classes/adult-lessons/group-paddles/.

2. South Bay Trail

10th St and Taylor Ave to Boulevard Park
Bellingham, WA

You have several options as to where to park for the next two stops on this trip.

The full South Bay Trail is 2.5 miles long (one way), running from E Maple St and Railroad Ave in Bellingham to 10th St and Mill Ave in Fairhaven. However, a unique half-mile (one way) section of the trail is on an elevated boardwalk over the bay (Bellingham Bay). The views can't be beat, and on a sunny day the breeze from the water makes for a perfect short walk, accessible for all people.

I recommend parking in Fairhaven near 10th St and Mill Ave (official address: Mill Ave & 10th St, Bellingham, WA 98225), a good base for the South Bay Trail and then the next stop on the trip, downtown Fairhaven. However, if you park at 10th St and Mill Ave, you'll add on a little more than a third of a mile each way to your walk on the South Bay Trail.

If you or people you are with have trouble walking that extra distance, you have two other options: (1) park at the south end of the boardwalk, at the intersection of 10th St and Taylor Ave (at historic Taylor Dock, the beginning of the half-mile section); or (2) park at the north end of the half-mile section, in Boulevard Park. The Boulevard Park parking lot is not terribly large, though, and on sunny days you almost certainly will have trouble parking there. 10th St and Taylor Ave can be busy, too, but nearby parking is easier to find.

Wherever you decide to park, make your way to the South Bay Trail and take a stroll along the elevated boardwalk. At the Boulevard Park end, grab a coffee at the popular Woods Coffee on the waterfront.

3. Downtown Fairhaven

Fairhaven was founded in the late 1880s, and newly constructed buildings are now required to conform to the iconic 19th-century look and style the area is known for. The downtown core is chock-full of artsy shops and galleries, tantalizing restaurants, fun places for happy hour, and much more.

Make your own way around town, dipping into whatever stores suit your fancy. Be sure to find the amazingly realistic mural in the courtyard outside Village Books, at the Fairhaven Village Green (near 10th St and Mill Ave)!

Some ideas include:

Village Books
1200 11th Street
Bellingham, WA 98225
(360) 671-2626
www.villagebooks.com
"Three floors of new, used, and bargain books." A favorite of book lovers from all over the area.

Good Earth Pottery
1000 Harris Ave
Bellingham, WA 98225
(360) 671-3998
www.goodearthpots.com
Representing more than fifty local artists.

Paper Dreams
1200 11th Street
Bellingham, WA 98225
(360) 676-8676
www.paperdreamsfairhaven.com
Greeting cards, novelty gifts, puzzles and games, and more.

The Garden Room
1006 Harris Ave # 120
Bellingham, WA 98225
(360) 734-9949
www.gardenroomfairhaven.com
Tropical plants, elegant home and garden décor, French jewelry, and great gifts for your friends and family.

Whimsey
1001 Harris Ave
Bellingham, WA 98225
(360) 733-5568
www.shopwhimsey.com
Designer jewelry, art, and gifts from many local and regional artists.

Rocket Donuts
1021 Harris Ave
Bellingham, WA 98225
(360) 366-8135
www.rocketdonuts.com
Serving donuts, espresso, and also Acme ice cream made in nearby Acme, WA. And it's also a sci-fi movie museum!

Colophon Cafe
1208-B 11th Street
Bellingham, WA 98225
360) 647-0092
www.colophoncafe.com
Delicious food, with outside dining available in a gorgeous court-yard.

Galloway's Cocktail Bar
1200 10th St Suite 102
Bellingham, WA 98225
(360) 756-2795
www.gallowayscocktail.bar
"Fairhaven's Deco Era Cocktail Bar" featuring great drinks and small bites.

Buildings of Primary Historical Significance include the following (read more about them at www.cob.org/services/planning/historic/Pages/fairhaven-district.aspx).

- Mason Block, 1200-1206 Harris Avenue
- Waldron Block, 1308-1314 12th Street
- Nelson Block, 1100-1102 Harris Avenue
- Terminal Building, 1101-1103 Harris Avenue
- Monahan Building, 1209 11th Street
- 1211 11th Street
- Knights of Pythias and Masonic Hall, 1208-1210 11th Street
- 1204-1206 11th Avenue
- Morgan Block, 1000-1002 Harris Avenue
- 913-915 Harris Avenue
- 909-911 Harris Avenue

- 1408-1410 11th Street
- Carnegie Library 1105 12th Street
- Kulshan Club, 1121 11th Street, 1120 Finnegan Way

Sites and Buildings of Secondary Historical Significance include the following:

- 1304-1306 11th Street
- 1112-1114 Harris Avenue
- 1111-1115 Harris Avenue

4. Chuckanut Drive Scenic Byway

Washington State Route 11, from Burlington to Bellingham

Sure, you could drive on I-5 and it would be faster, but Chuckanut Drive, a 21-mile scenic coastline drive along Chuckanut Bay, is not to be missed. This route winds and curves through the coastal forests, hugging the cliffs along the base of Chuckanut Mountain before veering inland toward the farmland flats. Viewpoints along the way allow you to pull over and get a good look, but watch out for cars parked on the tight shoulder, and keep your eyes open for bicyclists!

Chuckanut Drive is dotted with tons of great trails and parks. You'll undoubtedly want to return and spend more time in this area!

Optional Side Trips:

Larrabee State Park: Washington's first State Park (Discover Pass needed), with spectacular views of the San Juan Islands and Samish Bay. Hiking, biking, fishing, picnicking, more. parks.state. wa.us/536/Larrabee

Fairhaven Park: a multipurpose community park with picnic shelters, barbecue grills, playground, basketball court, and more. www.cob.org/ services/recreation/parks-trails/Pages/fairhaven-park.aspx

Interurban Trail: 6.7 miles, connecting Fairhaven to Larrabee State Park following a former electric rail line.

5. Chuckanut Manor and Sammy the Samish Bay Sea Monster

3056 Chuckanut Drive
Bow, WA
360-766-6191
www.chuckanutmanor.com

Getting hungry? Stop for a bite to eat or a cocktail, and be sure to grab a seat on the deck. Delicious food and great service with a spectacular view make this a favorite stop of mine when I'm in the area. What's more, from the deck, you may get a glimpse of Sammy the Samish Bay Sea Monster (who looks very much like he could be a relative of the Loch Ness Monster). Ask your server if there have been any sightings lately.

6. Downtown Edison

Note: plan your day so that you arrive in Edison before 5 p.m. when everything closes!

Continue down Chuckanut Drive and take a right on Bow Hill Road to land yourself in the tiny town ("census designated place") of Edison, WA. Edison has a history as a socialist/utopian community; in fact, Equity Colony, a national utopian socialist project, once had its headquarters there. The colony didn't last much past 1900 but the nouveau hippie vibe lives on. Today, the laid-back coastal community is home to artists and artisans, farmers, birders, and people looking for a slower way of life.

There's a bit of a transience to the retail community here. The shops lining the streets three years ago are not necessarily the shops of today, and may not be the shops three years from now. Still, there are no vacant lots or empty spaces. The town, however small—make that tiny, postage-stamp—is nonetheless vibrant. If you take the time to ask people their stories, they'll be more than happy to tell you what brought them to—or, in many places, back to—this community of less than 150 people.

Avoiding crowds can be difficult on summer weekends. In such a compact space, even a few dozen visitors can feel like a swarm. Parking may seem like a challenge, but as the proprietor of Hedgerow pointed out to me, in Seattle you park and walk farther in a Costco parking lot than you'll have to do in Edison.

To make the most of your visit, you'll want to be in town on a Friday, Saturday, or Sunday between the hours of 11 a.m. and 5 p.m.; many stores have limited days and hours. The "downtown" area itself is not much more than one street, Cains Ct, but the nearby residential streets are also fun for a stroll, overflowing with lush gardens and decorated with artistic touches as you'd expect in this sort of community.

On the side of The Lucky Dumpster, a mural recollects a famous quote from Edward R. Murrow, famed broadcast journalist from the late 30s through the early 60s, who went to Edison High School: "Anyone who isn't confused really doesn't understand the situation."

Some stops include:

Slough Food
5766 Cains Court Suite B
Edison, WA 98232
(360) 766.4458
www.sloughfood.com
Open Wednesday through Saturday 11 to 6; Sundays 11 to 5

John DeGloria, proprietor, is typical of the owners of the shops in Edison: delightful to talk to, and more than happy to give you his time and talk about his passion. In John's case, it's meats and cheeses. Pick up some picnic food here (and some delicious grocery treats for yourself, or perfect for host/hostess gifts). John describes his merchandise as: "food, wine and cheese made with care and integrity from small producers in regions off the beaten path." The eating space inside is small but comfortable. Be sure to check out the outside space, out the back door. There are several small tables scattered around—including a few you have to hunt for, through the gardens and overlooking Edison Slough. The tables nearest the building are protected by an overhead cover, and giant heaters will keep you cozy on cooler days.

The store occasionally hosts wine, cheese and chocolate tastings, as well as oyster parties and paella parties. Call for more information.

Smith & Vallee Gallery
5742 Gilkey Avenue
Edison, WA 98232
(360) 766-6230
www.smithandvalleegallery.com/gallery
Open every day, 11 to 5

Located in a light and airy restored school house, this gallery represents "the finest established and emerging artists across the Northwest and beyond." On my latest visit, the two featured artists were the owner and a staff member of the antique shop kitty-corner to the gallery. Very local indeed! Featured artists rotate every month.

Breadfarm
5766 Cains Court
Edison, WA 98232
(360) 766-4065
www.breadfarm.com
Open every day, 8 to 6

Cash and check only; no credit cards. "Artisan bakery focusing on naturally leavened breads, rustic pastry, and pantry staples." The retail space is small but the food is yummy. For a treat, check out the melt-in-your mouth graham crackers.

Hedgerow
5787 Cains Ct
Edison, WA 98232
(206) 605.8639
www.hedgerowedison.com
Open Friday, Saturday, and Sunday 11 to 5

A fun shop with cute merchandise and a fabulous and friendly owner. What does she sell? The website says, "stocking new, last decade, and last century" goods. Jewelry, clothing, vintage items, dishes, silverware, you name it.

Optional Side Trips:
Edison Bird Festival: The area is known for fantastic birdwatching. Therefore, in February of each year, the town hosts a festival focusing on the art and conservation of birds. And, of course, they top it off with a Chicken Parade, for which people of all ages gather in chicken costumes and chicken hats and all things chicken. www. facebook.com/edisonbirdfestival/

Bird Watching: Pretty much the whole area is great for avian enthusiasts, but a great spot for hiking and bird watching is Bay View State Park on Padilla Bay. parks.state.wa.us/473/Bay-View.

Dancing at The Old Edison Inn: A great place for grass-fed beef burgers or fried local oysters, but also, if your feet were made for dancing, you'll want to check this place out. Twice voted by Cascadia Weekly Magazine as the best place for dancing, The Old Edison Inn has live music and dancing Saturday nights at 8:30, and Sunday nights at 5:30. www.theoldedison.com, 5829 Cains Court.

7. Samish Bay Cheese

15115 Bow Hill Rd
Bow, WA 98232
(360) 766-6707
www.samishbay.com
Open every day, but hours vary (generally 10 to 4/5/6); check website.

The signage of Samish Bay Cheese is easy to miss, so key the address into your GPS and keep your eyes open for low-lying off-white buildings with a deep rust-colored trim.

Samish Bay Cheese is much more than a cheese shop. (As they say, it's "Samish Bay Cheese & Whey More." Get it?) A map available at the retail shop (open 363 days a year) will lead you on a self-guided tour of the feeding alley, talking fields, production building, pasture, and more. During open hours you are welcome to try a variety of cheeses, almost all of which they make on site. Along with the cheeses they sell yogurts and kefir. They also fill growlers and sell wine, and offer a wide range of organic meats, including a variety of "weird meat cuts" (as described by Austin, a friendly and helpful employee). Because they raise their own pork and beef, every bit of the animal is available for purchase, from tongue and other organ meats, to beef and soup and marrow bones, to jowls—or as Austin called it, "face bacon." The store also sells rendered lard, which Austin told me is spectacular in pie crust, and makes the best tortillas.

8. Bow Hill Blueberries

15628 Bow Hill Road
Bow, WA 98232
(360) 399-1006
www.bowhillblueberries.com
Open Monday through Saturday 10 to 5; Sundays 11 to 5

Finish off your day with one last farm stop, at Bow Hill Blueberries. From early July through Labor Day, you can U-pick blueberries in their field, or buy them fresh in the store. All year long, the store is still open with blueberries in all forms: frozen berries, blueberry ice cream, blueberry juice, blueberry sauce, pickled blueberries, blueberry jam, blueberry powder and more.

Optional Side Trip:
A peaceful, easy feeling: If you delight in the rural look and feel of barns and farms, on your way home, take some time to drive aimlessly amongst the various fields.

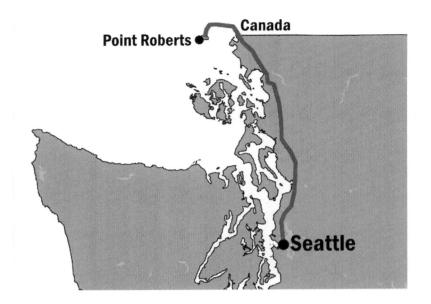

Stops:

1. Point Roberts International Marketplace
2. Scenic Loop Part I + Fire Hydrants
3. Lily Point Marine Park
4. Lighthouse Marine Park
5. Kiniski's Reef Tavern
6. Monument Park
7. Blue Heron Gallery
8. Auntie Pam's Country Store

Point Roberts

Point Roberts is one of fourteen exclaves in the United States. This five-square-mile piece of land is part of the US, but to get there (via land) you have to go through Canada.

Total miles driven: 280
Left home: 8:00 a.m.
Returned home: 4:30 p.m.

After I decided to include Point Roberts in this book, of course the next step was to visit. Here's how my border crossing (US to Canada) on my first trip went down:

Canadian Border Crossing Agent: "Where are you going?"
Me: "Point Roberts."
CBCA: "What are you going for?"
Me: "I'm writing a book about Day Trips from Seattle, and I'm going to include it."
CBCA: "Point Roberts?" A tiny smile escapes through his professional guard facade. "That'll be a short chapter."

Once I got over the simple pleasure of making a border crossing agent smile, I smugly thought to myself, "Oh, I'll find things to do. I'm Pam! Pam on the Map! I can find things to do anywhere!"

But the border crossing agent was not completely wrong. Though the area seems to be a lovely place to live, this is not a place one visits for excitement, unless you time your trip to coincide with a festival or their popular 4th of July parade and associated festivities. This is a place to come to get away from it all, rest, walk, bike, and relax.

Point Roberts, or "Point Bob" or "the Point," is interesting more as a talking point and conversation piece than as an exciting destination. Back in 1846 when the UK and the US signed the Oregon Treaty, after years of debate on the US-Canadian border they settled on the 49th parallel. However, someone wasn't looking at a map at the time, and forgot about Point Roberts. This tiny tip of the Tsawwassen Peninsula became a land exclave of the United States. Driving to Point Roberts from the US means crossing into Canada first, then back across the border.

[Note: there are enclaves, exclaves, and pene-exclaves. And some places that are exclaves of one state/country are enclaves of other states/countries...? Furthermore, some of what I'm reading says Point Roberts is not an exclave but actually a pene-exclave. So while Point Roberts is a U.S. pene-exclave (I think), it is also Canada's American enclave. I'll be honest, trying to figure out the differences between all of the above are twisting my mind into knots. Alaska is also a pene-exclave, apparently, but Hawaii is a Federal enclave. Got it??]

Just over 1,300 people call Point Roberts home. Do they consider themselves Canadian, or U.S. Residents? The people I talked to generally felt a little bit of both, but maybe mostly neither. They're from Point Roberts, and that's that. Word on the street is that at any given time there are about eighty-five people in the witness protection program living there—a border crossing point makes Point Roberts far more secure than any restraining order could. There are also a good number of people of Icelandic origin; the area was originally settled in the late 19th century by Icelandic fishermen.

Point Roberts is not a place one goes to "do" so much as it is a place to "be." If you visit, don't expect flashy entertainment and non-stop action. Rather, expect to slow down. Breathe. Relax.

Note: Once you've crossed the border, you might wonder, "What are all these parcel service companies?" As it turns out, it's much cheaper to mail things to and from the U.S. than it is from Canada. Therefore, Canadians who live near Point Roberts use these services to mail and pick up packages. (This is also part of why there could be a much longer line crossing the border into Point Roberts than you expected. A lot of those people are just going to get their mail.) Point Roberts is, in fact, the fifth busiest crossing on the US/Canada border, with more than a million people crossing in and out each year.

Officially, Point Roberts is an unincorporated zone without city status, and is a part of Whatcom County. I asked the clerk at Auntie Pam's Country Store whether it was a town or city or something else, and he told me, "It's a socio-geopolitical anomaly." Whatever it is, this community is tight-knit. If someone in Point Roberts needs help, the others in Point Roberts will be there.

Passes required:

No park or forest passes are required, but don't leave home without your passport!

Important notes:

Roads and driving: When you hit Canada, don't forget the speed limit signs are all in kilometers per hour. I like Rick Steves' rough method of converting: take the number in KPH, halve it, and add back ten percent:

100 KPH: half of 100 = 50; ten percent = 10,
    so 100 KPH is about 50+10, or 60 MPH
60 KPH: half of 60 = 30; ten percent = 6,
    so 60 KPH is about 30+6, or 36 MPH
50 KPH: half of 50 = 25; ten percent = 5,
    so 50 KPH is about 25+5, or 30 MPH

Gas: Whenever I'm heading north on a road trip, I like to stop for gas in Arlington (exit 208). Point Roberts is known for cheap gas, but that's only relative to the prices in Canada. People from Canada like to cross the border to fuel up, but you might want to get your gas somewhere along the way. When I stopped in Arlington for my day trip to Point Roberts, I paid $2.51 at the cheapest place. Gas in Point Roberts was $2.91 on that same day. Don't be fooled when the gas prices look insanely cheap, because Canadians are used to seeing prices listed by liter rather than gallon, the gas stations in Point Roberts also list their prices by liter. Therefore, the $0.77 per liter price I saw converted to $2.91 per gallon. This was still a much better price than across the border. The Point Roberts gas station also listed the prices in Canadian dollars: $0.99 CDN per liter. On the Canadian side, the gas was $1.33 CDN per liter. Regardless of exchange rate, that makes for a very good savings when crossing the border.

My point being: gas up in the U.S., whether Point Roberts or somewhere along I-5 on the way up.

Food: Remember you're crossing the border four times on this trip—twice going and twice coming. To avoid hassle at the borders, just don't bring food along.

Credit card and currency: Since technically part of this day trip is an international trip, and having your credit card refused can ruin a good day, you might want to notify your credit card company that you'll be out of the area. Once you're in Point Roberts, I'm told most stores have both a U.S. till and a Canadian till, meaning they can accept cash in either currency. Or you can just use your credit card!

Cell phone / internet: As you drive through Canada be aware that you very likely are out of your mobile plan. Personally, I turn off my phone at the border just in case. Once you're in Point Roberts, I'm told Verizon is the only carrier that has service there, but even with Verizon as my carrier, I still had limited coverage.

Getting there:

Grab your passport and head north. Around milepost 250, keep your eyes open for a sign that will tell you current wait times at the various local border crossings. The rest area after milepost 267 is a good place to stop and turn your phone to airplane mode (unless you're not worried about incurring international roaming charges). It's also a good place to stop and actually use the rest room, in case you find yourself in a very long line at the border.

(At U.S. Exit 275, you can follow signs to a different, and sometimes less busy, border crossing. However, I think the Peace Arch border crossing is easiest for this particular trip as it keeps you on the correct road.)

Cross into Canada, and stay on BC-99. Follow BC-99 N to Exit 26 toward BC-17. Keep right and follow signs to 17/Tsawwassen. After about 5 miles, use one of the two left lanes to turn left onto 56th St. Follow this road to the border crossing back into the U.S., where the road becomes Tyee Dr. Drive just over a mile until you see the International Market on your left. (See below Stop #1.)

Stops:

1. Point Roberts International Marketplace
2. Scenic Loop Part I + Fire Hydrants
3. Lily Point Marine Park
4. Lighthouse Marine Park
5. Kiniski's Reef Tavern
6. Monument Park
7. Blue Heron Gallery
8. Auntie Pam's Country Store

Optional Side Trip:
Peace Arch Historical State Park: (parks.state.wa.us/562/Peace-Arch) The last U.S. exit before the border is Exit 276; taking it will take you into the Peace Arch Park. This 20-acre day-use park is technically two parks, one in the U.S. and one in Canada. (The park on the Canadian side is Peace Arch Provincial Park.) Wander along about half a mile of trails, or stop for a picnic at one of the 85 picnic tables.

1. Point Roberts International Marketplace

480 Tyee Drive
Point Roberts, WA 98281
(360) 945-0237
www.pointrobertsmarketplace.com

As discussed, your GPS might not be working well here, but fear not! It's very easy to find a map. When you cross the border, you're now on Tyee Road. Continue on Tyee Road to the first "big" road, Gulf Road (Benson Road will be the first road, on your right; then Gulf Road is the next right). As you approach Gulf Road, the Marketplace will be on your left. Pull in and get yourself a Point Roberts map. You can get these at almost any store, restaurant, or other public place in town.

Optional Side Trip:
Rent a bike: With its varied terrain and light traffic, Point Roberts is great for biking. In fact, one resident told me that when the Olympics were in Vancouver, cyclists from all over the world came and trained in Point Roberts. If you want to tour the town from atop two wheels rather than four, head next to Pedal Pushers Bikes (1356 Gulf Rd, Point Roberts, WA 98281; www.facebook.com/PedalPushersBikes) and rent a bike. They're not open every day, so check ahead if bicycling is in your plan.

2. Scenic Loop Part I + Fire Hydrants

Start at the intersection of Tyee Road and Johnson Road and head east

Let's be honest, you can't get too lost in a five-square-mile area surrounded on three sides by water and one side by a border crossing. However, until you get your bearings, it's easy to get turned around. For the sake of getting your bearings, and to get an overview of the lay of the land, take the Scenic Loop Drive. I recommend driving it clockwise, backtracking now along Tyee Road to Johnson Road; right on Johnson Road and continuing to Boundary Bay Road.

While you're driving, watch for fire hydrants. Back in 2013, the Fire Chief noticed that the fire hydrants were all getting tired and weary; however, as is often the case with budgets, there was no budget to hire someone to re-paint them all. Being a resourceful and creative-minded man, he announced a fire-hydrant-painting competition, inviting residents to use paint and supplies provided by the Fire Department and create their own fire hydrant masterpieces. Prizes were offered, and the residents took up the challenge with gusto. Now, almost every hydrant is painted with unique whimsy. Check them out as you drive along!

3. Lily Point Marine Park

2315 APA Road
Point Roberts, WA 98281
www.co.whatcom.wa.us/2099/Lily-Point-Marine-Park

At the end of Boundary Bay Road (but not the end of the Scenic Loop) you'll see the entrance to Lily Point Marine Park. Of the town's "four corners" parks, this is the largest, with 275 acres of land waiting to be explored. If you're in the mood, diverge from the Scenic Loop and head in for a hike or to check out the 1.4 miles of shoreline along Boundary Bay and the spectacular cliffs down at the beach.

4. Lighthouse Marine Park

811 Marine Dr
Point Roberts, WA 98281
www.co.whatcom.wa.us/1956/Lighthouse-Marine-Park

Get back on the APA Road and follow it west to its end; turn left onto Marina Dr and follow it as it becomes Edwards Dr. As it curves again, it becomes Marine Dr. (Yes, I swear that's right: Marina Dr on the east, Marine Dr on the west.) Take a left into another of the four corners parks, Lighthouse Marine Park. From here you can beachcomb and enjoy the fresh air and serenity, or walk the short perimeter trail. When winds are high, watch the battle between the waves and the sectional dock that bobs and crashes in the water. The area is home to three pods of Orca whales; signs indicate that this park is a good spot for whale watching. Keep your eyes open, and check out the two-story tower built just for the purpose. A large picnic area is available if you've brought a snack. Restrooms here are generally clean and well-maintained.

5. Kiniski's Reef Tavern

1334 Gulf Rd
Point Roberts, WA 98281
(360) 945-4042
www.facebook.com/KiniskisReefPointRoberts

Get back on Marine Dr and head north. There are a handful of places to eat in Point Roberts, but for the best view, stop at Kiniski's Reef Tavern and have a cocktail out on the patio. Standard tavern fare awaits you, but the view can't be beat, and chances are high you'll find your heart rate dropping a bit as you stare out at the waves.

6. Monument Park

25 Marine Dr
Point Roberts, WA 98281
www.co.whatcom.wa.us/2127/Monument-Park

At the northwestern most corner of Point Roberts is Monument Park. Here you'll find the most northwesterly boundary marker in the continental U.S., at latitude 49.0.0, longitude 123.3.53. Erected in 1861, it is one of more than 8,000 boundary markers that were laid down in the 1800s all along the U.S./Canada border.

Incidentally, if you don't remember this from school, the 5,525-mile-long border between the U.S. and Canada (including the 1,538-mile-long Alaska/Canada border) is the longest international border in the world. (The border between Washington and Canada is 427 miles long.) What's perhaps more interesting is that all along that 5,525-mile-long border, there's a 20-foot-wide treeless zone between the countries—known as "the slash," and maintained every six years by the International Boundary Commission (IBC).

It's odd to see the US/Canada border here: it's just a curb, and a sign telling people not to cross. Houses on the Canadian side are built almost right up to the border. It's easy to feel here that a country border is nothing more than an arbitrary, imaginary line.

A sometimes steep trail through the woods on the south side of the park leads down to the beach.

7. Blue Heron Gallery

1360 Gulf Rd
Point Roberts, WA 98281
(360) 945-2747

Stop by Blue Heron Gallery to see if they're open; hours and days are limited, but if they're open, it's worth a stop. Blue Heron Gallery is a casual, friendly gallery with a variety of handcrafted and local arts, crafts, jewelry, and more. Even if it's closed when you stop by, the fun and whimsical art outside the building will delight you.

8. Auntie Pam's Country Store

1480 Gulf Rd
Point Roberts, WA 98281
(360) 945-1626
www.auntiepams.com

Being an Auntie Pam myself, of course I had to stop in at this store, and you should too. Pamala Sheppard, the "Pam" behind "Auntie Pam" started the store as a storefront from which to sell her own handmade body care products such as soaps and sprays. She expanded to include all manner of quirky, fun, and interesting items, from clothing to organic groceries to tea to toys and more. Neighborhood kids stop by frequently to pick up some "penny" candy with their spare change.

Remember on heading home that crossing two borders again can take some time. On the last crossing, from Canada back into the US, I find that being in the left lane as you enter the border crossing area is your best bet for a shorter crossing. What starts as two lanes branches out into four or more, but somehow the right lane stays the right lane and the left lane diverges out into all the other lanes—which means it will move faster. However, I don't guarantee it!

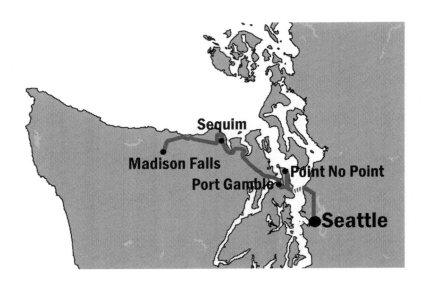

Stops:

1. Edmonds Ferry Terminal / Edmonds–Kingston Ferry
2. Point No Point Lighthouse
3. Port Gamble
4. Purple Haze Organic Lavender Farm
5. Graysmarsh Berry Farm
6. Downtown Sequim
7. Madison Falls
8. Harbinger Winery
9. Ferry home

Sequim

Home to the longest natural land spit in the nation, Sequim is widely known for its sunshine and lavender. (P.S. If you're not familiar with the town: it's pronounced "skwim." Really!)

Total miles driven: 192
Total miles on the ferry: 12
Left home: 7:20 a.m.
Returned home: 6:00 p.m.

This trip is great for relaxing, landscape photography, a scenic ferry ride, fresh produce, lovely calming scents, beach combing, nature walks, and wildlife viewing—with a hot springs option at the end!

Pronounced "skwim," Sequim is a word from the Klallam language meaning a place to go to hunt; a prairie. (The Klallam are four related Native American communities in the Pacific Northwest.)

In 2017, USA Today awarded Sequim the title of "Best Northwestern Small Town," beating out other Washington favorites, Port

Townsend, La Conner, Winthrop, and Friday Harbor. Sequim is also one of the sunniest spots in Western Washington, benefitting from the rain shadow effect of the Olympic Mountains. On average, Sequim gets only about 16 inches of rain per year.

Once an area considered to be an agricultural powerhouse, these days, Sequim is famous for its lavender farms. It is, in fact, the Lavender Capital of North America®, complete with the ®! Lavender blooms from mid-June-ish through mid-September-ish. The Sequim Lavender Festival takes over the purple town in late July, generally the third weekend of July, Friday through Sunday.

Do I recommend you visit during the festival? That depends on how you feel about crowds. If, like me, you don't love crowds, just visit the lavender farms during lavender season, but skip the festival weekend. If you go on a weekday, there are far fewer visitors, parking is easier, and you can get pictures without a million people. (Festival information: www.lavenderfestival.com.)

Don't think your choices are limited to festival weekends, though. Sequim is very tourism-forward, and the town has events going on year-round.

Passes required:

None

Important notes:

Ferry: Ferries are both fabulous and unpredictable. If you take this trip on a weekend day, you'll likely have longer lines in the morning than if you go Monday through Friday. Coming back, there's a good chance you'll have to wait longer as well. Pack your patience. Get a round trip ticket (unless you plan to drive the long way around either going or coming).

Food: As this is an agricultural area, there are plenty of produce stands. If you think you might purchase berries or other produce on this trip, it's not a bad idea to bring containers to put them in. Staining the interior of your car (or even just the trunk) with the juice of delicious raspberries, blackberries, and blueberries is not great for resale value!

Getting there:

Head north to the Edmonds–Kingston Ferry. Take the ferry to Kingston and get on WA-104 West. Detours as noted below.

I prefer the Edmonds–Kingston Ferry because my starting point is farther north. However, the Seattle–Bainbridge Island Ferry is also an option, if that is closer to your starting point and/or more convenient. Either way, follow your GPS!

Alternatively, if you don't want to take the ferry, you can take I-5 South to Tacoma, then get on WA-16 West, then WA-3 North, then WA-104 West. (You'll have to detour off this route to get to Point No Point.) Surprisingly, this route adds less than an hour (in theory), and also avoids the uncertainty of ferry line wait times.

Stops:

1. Edmonds Ferry Terminal / Edmonds–Kingston Ferry
2. Point No Point Lighthouse
3. Port Gamble
4. Purple Haze Organic Lavender Farm
5. Graysmarsh Berry Farm
6. Downtown Sequim
7. Madison Falls
8. Harbinger Winery
9. Ferry home

NOTE: Since this is an out-and-back route, you can do these in whatever order you like.

1. Edmonds Ferry Terminal / Edmonds-Kingston Ferry

199 Sunset Ave S
Edmonds, WA 98020
www.wsdot.com/ferries

Check the WSDOT website for ferry times, and plan your arrival at the terminal accordingly. If you're not familiar with ferry wait times, your best bet is to give yourself plenty of time and be prepared to wait for a second boat (less likely on weekdays, more likely on weekends, especially if you aren't planning an early start). For the 7:55 a.m. ferry on a weekday, I made the (accurate) assumption that ferry traffic would not be heavy in the Edmonds-to-Kingston direction, so we arrived around 7:40 and had no trouble getting on.

The actual ferry travel time from Edmonds to Kingston is a little less than 30 minutes: enough time to get out of your car, go up on deck, and, weather depending, check out the fantastic views.

A point of interest: the Washington state ferry system is currently the largest ferry system in the U.S. On the day of my research trip, we were on the "Spokane," one of the state ferry system's "Jumbo Class" ferries, carrying up to 2,000 passengers and 206 cars (depending on type and size).

After you exit the ferry, for a short distance both left and right lanes continue; then the left lane merges into the right. Since you're exiting with ferry traffic (obviously), you'll be stuck in ferry traffic for a bit until you turn right onto Hansville Road. (Most of the traffic will continue straight at that point.)

Photo Op #1:

About 6.1 miles after you turn right onto Hansville Road, watch on your right: someone has taken a giant round object (I'm sure some of you will know what it is, but I don't) and painted a happy face on it. Sure to cheer you up!

Photo Op #2:

Less than half a mile after you turn onto Point No Point Road, watch on your right for the "ship house." It's actually made out of the top of a tugboat that was used in WWII by the U.S. Maritime Commission, and brought to Hansville in 1972 to begin its service as a home on land.

2. Point No Point Lighthouse

9009 Point No Point Rd NE
Hansville, WA 98340
www.pnplighthouse.com

Point No Point Lighthouse is a gorgeous, squatty little lighthouse on Puget Sound, with a fantastic beach on which you can stroll for miles (depending on tide). If you're there at a slow time, you'll wonder why there's so much overflow parking and warnings in the neighborhood not to park on private neighborhood streets. If you're there at a busy time, you'll understand.

There are picnic benches on the upper stretches of the beach, or you can bring your own chair (or beach towel) and stay a while. This is a favorite spot for fishermen and fisherwomen, who gather in abundance in the morning anchoring their boats just off the shore, or even fish from the beach itself.

If you've walked straight to the beach from the parking lot, as you're looking out toward the water and a bit to the right (north-east), that pure snow-capped mountain across the water is Mount Baker. Turn around, and Mount Rainier is straight across from the parking lot in the other direction (south and a little east).

No pass is needed.

3. Port Gamble

Map coordinates: 47.854201, -122.584131

Port Gamble is a tiny town with literally only about two dozen streets—and that's being generous about what you call a street and including every side road as well. Still, if you've not been here (or even if you have), it's worth a stop. The town emerged as a com-pany town: a community born to support the sawmill founded by William Talbot and Anthony Pope in 1853. The sawmill was in operation until 1995, which at the time made it the longest contin-uously operating mill in the U.S. In 1996, Pope Resources commit-ted to refurbishing the town; today the houses, public areas, ceme-tery, etc., are currently all maintained by Olympic Property Group.

With this commitment, this town (technically "unincorporat-ed community") is the epitome of "quaint." For such a small place, it has an exceptionally high ratio of shops full of things you sud-denly discover you can't live without. Walk into the Port Gamble General Store and Café at your own risk: you'll find treasures in-side that you simply must have. If a friend's birthday is coming up, or you're shopping for Christmas or other holidays, I can al-most guarantee you'll find something here for several people on your list. And of course there are items you yourself must have, too! Consider yourself warned. I also love Wish, another shop that seems tiny on the outside but spreads to include multiple rooms on the inside.

Hungry? Grab a snack at Mrs. Muir's House Tearoom & Treasures, or pick up something quick and easy at the General Store. Or, check out Butcher & Baker Provisions—it sounds like a place to buy meat and flour, but in fact is a café and deli with loads of delicious items on the menu.

As a final stop, walk up to the Buena Vista Cemetery, overlooking the water, off Walker Street between Kitsap Ave and Puget Way. Check out the amazing view, and the weathered headstones dating back to 1856, when the cemetery was established. And, keep an eye out for ghosts ... this is one of Port Gamble's reportedly many haunted sites.

Ghost Alert:
If ghost hunting and things that go bump in the night excite you, some say Port Gamble is the place to be, overflowing with the no-longer-living. The Walker-Ames House, a historic home from when the Port Gamble Mill was active, is particularly well known these days for (supposed) paranormal sightings. It is now a hotspot for ghost hunters, and has been the site of reports of paranormal activity since the 1950s. Some say it is the most haunted house in Washington's most haunted town. You can decide for yourself! If you're in town between October and March, check into a special investigation tour. Find out more at Port Gamble Paranormal, www.portgambleparanormal.com.

Photo Op:
Back en route to Sequim, maybe 3.5-ish miles after 104 meets up with 101, you'll pass through the tiny hamlet of Discovery Bay. As you do, on your right there are some repurposed railway cars, painted in bright cheerful colors. (According to Google maps, the address is 282023 Olympic Hwy, Port Townsend, WA.) It looks

like a marijuana shop might now be calling the rail cars home, but they're nonetheless worthy of a picture.

4. Purple Haze Organic Lavender Farm

180 Bell Bottom Rd
Sequim, WA 98382
360-683-1714
www.purplehazelavender.com

As I mentioned, Sequim is now known largely for its Lavender Festival in summer, but its lavender industry is a focal point year-round. More than a dozen lavender farms dot the landscape in the greater Sequim area, and many of them also have shops downtown for those who don't want to go out to the fields.

Take your pick of the various farms, or visit more than one if you can't get enough. Purple Haze Organic Lavender Farm, now entering its third decade, is one of my favorites.

Photographers, bring all your lenses, for everything from wide shots to extreme close-ups. During lavender season, even amateur photographers will find themselves spending a good bit of time framing the perfect photo of the purple flowers, the drunk-happy bees, the bright red ladybugs hopping gleefully from stem to stem. With a bright blue sky as a backdrop and the aroma of this fragrant herb calming all your senses, you will want to stay a while. And re-member, the farms are not only open the weekend of the Festival; many are open all year long.

Purple Haze spreads out over twelve acres, with more than 15,000 plants in more than fifty varieties. Wandering the fields, the air saturated with the gentle scent of lavender, the happy bees humming with joy, is a calming experience like none other.

Other farms include:
- Washington Lavender
- Nelson's Duckpond & Lavender Farm
- Lost Mountain Lavender
- Jardin Du Soleil Lavender
- Earth Muffin Lavender
- Martha Lane Lavender
- Kitty B Lavender Farm
- And several more!

5. Graysmarsh Berry Farm

6187 Woodcock Road
Sequim, WA 98382
www.graysmarsh.com
Call (360) 683-5563 during the summer for the latest recorded U-Pick information.

For me, summer means berries. Whether raspberries are your favorites (as they are mine), or strawberries, or blueberries, or more, there's nothing like the ripe, sweet taste of local berries on a warm summer day. Head to Graysmarsh Berry Farm to pick your own, or buy pre-picked berries on site. As with almost all farms in the area, Graysmarsh also features lovely lavender to look at or to purchase in bundles.

6. Downtown Sequim

Map coordinates: 48.083968, -123.102335

I'm not going to lie. After quaint, adorable Port Gamble, can any other downtown really compare? Downtown Sequim isn't as quaint or adorable, even if it did win that USA Today award. Nonetheless, while you're here, it's worth a drive through to get a feel for the town, and maybe pick up a snack if you're hungry. If you haven't had the chance to buy lavender-related goods, several stores in town can help you fill all your lavender needs. Wander around, and see if you can find a hidden gem to make this your own favorite place.

Sequim-Area Off-Season / Non-Lavender Options
If you visit Sequim and its surrounding area outside lavender season, there's still plenty to do. According to www.visitsunnysequim. com, there are special wine tasting events in February, May, and November; a BirdFest/BirdQuest in April; Riverfest in September; the North Olympic Fiber Arts Festival in October; First Friday Art Walks throughout the year; and weekly Bird Walks every Wednesday morning.

Optional Side Trips:
Dungeness National Wildlife Refuge
554 Voice of America Road
Sequim, WA 98382
www.fws.gov/refuge/dungeness
$3 daily entrance fee per family or group (up to four adults). Also accepts a variety of passes. Established more than 100 years ago as

a refuge, preserve, and breeding ground for native birds, this is a beautiful area for hiking, photography, and wildlife viewing.

Dungeness Spit and Lighthouse
At 5.5 miles long, the Dungeness Spit is the longest natural sand spit in the nation. If you're thinking about hiking it, note that the path is uneven, taking you over endless shifting and wobbly large rocks. Even well-seasoned hikers can find it challenging. Be careful about your ankles and knees! Access this spit through the Dungeness National Wildlife Refuge.

Olympic Game Farm
1423 Ward Road
Sequim, WA 98382
(360) 683-4295
www.olygamefarm.com
Get up close with bison, bears, bobcats, wolves, deer, llamas, yaks, and more at the Olympic Game Farm. Drive through the farm's eighty-four acres and experience wildlife from the comfort and safety of your vehicle.

Happy Valley Alpaca Ranch
4629 Happy Valley Road
Sequim, WA 98382
(360) 681-0948
www.happyvalleyalpacaranch.com
Linda and Mike Gooch have been raising and breeding alpacas for twenty years. Take a free ranch tour, visit the alpacas (and one llama), and stop by the store to buy yarn, fiber, alpaca products, gifts, and more.

Dungeness River Audubon Center and Railroad Bridge Park
2151 West Hendrickson Road
PO Box 2450
Sequim, WA 98382
(360) 681-4076
www.dungenessrivercenter.org
Get out into nature to view the local flora and fauna with a walk on this historic bridge and trestle, or along the nature trails trails along the river's edge, and check out the educational and interpretive exhibits at the Audobon Center.

7. Madison Creek Falls Trailhead (and Falls)

(Also known as Madison Falls)
Olympic Hot Springs Road off Highway 101
just before Elwha, WA
Map coordinates: 48.041081, -123.590257
www.wta.org/go-hiking/hikes/madison-falls

If you love waterfalls as I do, for a (very) short hike with a nice reward, check out Madison Creek Falls. This trail is accessible for almost everyone.

To get to the falls, head out Highway 101 toward Elwha. Just before Elwha there's a brown sign to the Olympic National Park and Elwha Valley. That's Hot Springs Road, which is the road you want. Head down the road until you get to a parking lot that is very clearly marked for Madison Creek Falls.

Cars park somewhat haphazardly here. The trailhead is off to the left, and there's an outhouse there as well. Just past the outhouse are the remnants of a stump of a very old tree, with another little tree growing out of the edge. The original tree was maybe nine or ten feet in diameter, but now is just a shell of its former self, with the inside completely hollowed out. Photo op!

Stroll the 200 meters down to the falls and enjoy! (Note: I've seen several distances listed for the trail, anywhere from 200 feet to 1/10 mile. Regardless, it's short, and more or less level; a very easy walk.)

The river across from the parking lot is the Elwha, and also makes for a lovely breathing space.

Optional Side Trips:

Sol Duc Hot Springs: If you're still energized, keep going on to Mineral Hot Springs and Pool at Sol Duc Hot Springs Resort. Take a dip in one of three mineral hot springs pools or one freshwater pool. Mineral pools range from about 99°F to 104°F; the freshwater pool is a cooler 55°F to 85°F. Fees apply. 12076 Sol Duc Hot Springs Rd., Port Angeles, WA 98363, www.olympicnationalparks.com/things-to-do/mineral-hot-springs-pool-at-sol-duc-hot-springs-resort/.

Lake Crescent and Marymere Falls: The crystal clear waters of Lake Crescent make this another popular spot, and the hike to two-tiered Marymere Falls is a mostly easy 1.8-mile (round trip) trail leaving from Storm King Ranger Station. Historic Lake Crescent Lodge was built in 1915, and features a dining room overlooking the lake, open late April through December.

Olympic Discovery Trail: The 130-mile-long Olympic Discovery Trail passes through this area. If you've always dreamed of hiking the Pacific Coast Trail but would prefer something more accessible, check out this trail! Designed for use by walkers, bicyclists, wheelchairs, and even equestrians in some places, this wide, accessible trail connects communities across the north end of the peninsula. www.olympicdiscoverytrail.com, www.peninsulatrails-coalition.org.

Elwha Dam Removal: At this site in September 2011, the largest dam removal in U.S. history began. Now, the river is thriving. Find out more: www.nps.gov/olym/learn/nature/elwha-ecosystem-restoration.htm. Map coordinates: 48.095031, -123.556176.

8. Harbinger Winery

2358 Highway 101 West, US-101
Port Angeles, WA 98363
(360) 452-4262
www.harbingerwinery.com

What better way to cap off a day trip than with a bit of tasting at a lovely winery? Harbinger Winery has some delightful wines ($5 for six tastes), but more than that, has a really nice, friendly atmosphere. Kelly, who was serving up the drinks on the day I was there, is the perfect hostess, offering lively conversation about both the wines and the region.

Wineries come and go, so check before you head out to see if the one you're interested in is still open (or is open when you want to go). Other wineries in the area at the time of this writing include:

- Wind Rose Cellars, 143 W Washington, Sequim, WA 98382
- Olympic Cellars Winery, 255410 US-101, Port Angeles, WA 98362
- Camaraderie Cellars, 334 Benson Road, Port Angeles, WA 98363

See www.olympicpeninsulawineries.org for more information.

9. Take the ferry and head back home

Your day is done. Backtrack the way you came (or wander on a different route if you like) to the ferry. Get in line and wait. Be patient if necessary (you may have to wait for a ferry or two), load safely, and head home.

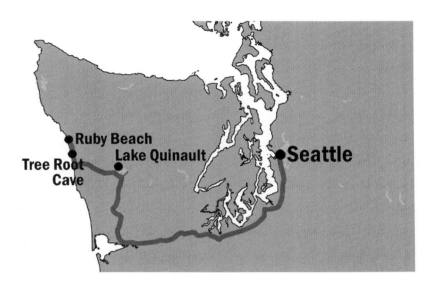

Stops:

1. Ruby Beach
2. Beach 4
3. Tree Root Cave
4. Merriman Falls
5. Big Spruce Tree (Largest Sitka Spruce Tree in the World)
6. Falls Creek Falls
7. Quinault Trail
8. Lake Quinault Lodge

Ruby Beach
and Lake Quinault

Some of the most beautiful beaches, forests, waterfalls, and trails in Washington are tucked up in the far northwestern edge. The area may be difficult to get to, but after you've been once you'll be dreaming about your next trip!

Total miles driven: 430
Left home: 7:00 a.m.
Returned home: 8:30 p.m.

In the day-to-day, north-to-south, I-5-corridor life of a person living in the Seattle area, it's easy to forget about the Olympic Peninsula. It's not on the way to anything or from anything; it's a place you arrive at intentionally. It's a destination, not a happenstance. Often overlooked and forgotten, the peninsula and its national park and forest, the aptly named Olympic National Park and Olympic National Forest, might be off your radar as far as day trips. That, however, is a mistake. The peninsula is overflowing with some of the most amazing places on earth—and it's all right at our doorstep.

I'll be honest. This road trip is long—probably too long. The driving alone is about seven and a half hours, and that's before you stop anywhere. You might well be tempted to skip out on some of the stops, which is fine. Ruby Beach alone is worth it, though, and my goal with this day trip is to get you out to the peninsula so you can see that you need to plan more time (a weekend, a few days) and go again soon. Think of this as an Olympic Peninsula Sampler Platter. Get a taste of what's out there, and decide what you want to try again next time.

This trip is for hiking, walking on the beach, admiring the forests, reflecting on lakes. Really, though, this trip is about awe. If you're a happiness junkie, as I am, reading about happiness all the time, you'll already know that one of the keys to being happy is regularly exposing yourself to situations in which you feel awe. (I could go into this much more, but you're not here for a discussion of happiness; you're here for a road trip!)

One way to tackle all these destinations would be to split up the itinerary into two days: take one day for the Ruby Beach and coastal spots, then another day for the trails and waterfalls around Lake Quinault.

Passes required:

The specific spots I've chosen for this itinerary do not require passes (but double check when you arrive in case I'm wrong or something has changed). However, if you go into other areas, some passes may be required. It's not a bad idea to take a handful of $5 bills with you to cover day use fees if needed.

Somewhat confusingly, the Olympic National Park and Olympic National Forest seem to blend together. As I understand it, the Olympic National Forest more or less encircles the Olympic

National Park. What this means is if you wander around, you might encounter a need for passes to both—once again making the America the Beautiful Annual Pass a great idea! www.nps.gov/planyourvisit/passes.htm.

Important notes:

Timing: Heading south from Seattle on a weekday you can't escape the work day commuters. Leaving early in the morning (like 7 or earlier) will be your best bet to make it through with the least amount of headaches.

Tides: It's hard to time tides with the days you have available for a road trip, but if you can, plan to go on a day where low tide will be a little before noon. This will mean the tide will be on its way out when you arrive, leaving you plenty of time to explore tide pools. www.nps.gov/olym/planyourvisit/tides-and-your-safety.htm.

Accessibility: To get to the actual beach at Ruby Beach, you will need to scramble over some driftwood. This may be difficult for people whose balance is not great, who have limited mobility, or for parents carrying children. (Sitting on a log and swinging your legs over often works!) The payoff is beyond worth it, but consider yourself warned. If you like to use hiking sticks, now might be a good time to bring them!

Gas: Once you're past Hoquiam, your options diminish severely. There's a station by Lake Quinault Lodge, another in Amanda Park (southwest edge of Lake Quinault), and another over in Queets at the coast. The Queets Trading Post also has public restrooms, which you may need by the time you get there!

Food: Definitely pack lunch and/or snacks for this trip. Your food options will become more and more scarce the farther you go.

Shoes: At the beach, you'll thank yourself if you bring flip flops or shoes that can get wet. After the beach, you'll thank yourself if you brought a spare dry pair of shoes and socks along, too!

Getting there:

Head south to Olympia on I-5, follow your GPS as the route meanders a bit, then take Highway 101 N.

Alternatively, if you wanted to make this a loop trip, you could start by going north to the Edmonds–Kingston Ferry, then taking Highway 104 to Highway 101 out to Ruby Beach. Depending on your starting point, the total travel time might be about the same.

Stops:

1. Ruby Beach
2. Beach 4
3. Tree Root Cave
4. Merriman Falls
5. Big Spruce Tree (Largest Sitka Spruce Tree in the World)
6. Falls Creek Falls
7. Quinault Trail
8. Lake Quinault Lodge

1. Ruby Beach

Highway 101
About milepost 164.5
Map coordinates: 47.707388, -124.413890

No pass required.

Get in the car early and drive, drive, drive all the way to Ruby Beach first. Parking is very limited and gets more crowded as the day goes on.

Be careful on your way down the trail from the parking lot. At the end of the trail, as noted above, you'll have to climb over some driftwood to get to the main part of the beach. Whatever you're carrying with you, make sure you're carrying it in bags or a backpack or something that will leave your hands free for balancing yourself as you make your way over the logs. (It's not too bad, really, but I want you to be prepared!)

Ruby Beach is not a place you go to sunbathe or swim. Ruby Beach is a place you go for the wilderness and the unmatched beauty, the tide pools, the bluffs, the sea stacks (or hay stacks, whatever you want to call them), the incomparable sunsets (not on this trip, though!), the long stretches of beach for walking and exploring and discovering. It is not uncommon for people to rate this as one of the best beaches they've ever seen. At low tide, it can feel like the beach is endless. There's something about being surrounded by vast open spaces and giant chunks of land that makes a person feel small, and sometimes feeling small is a good thing. It puts your troubles in perspective, and reminds you of the solidity of time.

You could easily spend your whole day here. Pack a picnic, some beach chairs, a book, and your sunscreen, and you're good to go until it's time to go home. However since we got you out here, let's explore some more...

Optional Side Trips:

Further on: You are achingly close to the Hoh Rain Forest and Second Beach (another spectacular favorite) now, both eminently worth visiting, but this day is already long. See what I mean? This is why you need to plan another visit sometime, a weekend or a few days rather than just a day trip.

Big Cedar Tree: Between Ruby Beach and Beach 4, you may still see signs for "Big Cedar Tree." This is one of two exceptionally notable cedar trees in the area that, unfortunately, have fallen in recent years. A storm in March 2014 split this particular tree in two; half collapsed to the ground. You can still follow the trail to see the tree, and there are many other worthy giants (trees, that is), in the area as well, but the thousand-year-old Big Cedar Tree the sign is referring to is in the process of returning to the earth. The other big cedar was the Quinault Big Cedar near the northwest shore of Lake Quinault. Before its demise, the Quinault tree was listed as the Largest Western Red Cedar in the world, was Washington's largest tree, and was the largest tree in the world outside of California. High winds in July 2016 put an end to the era of that tree, which was also estimated to be about a thousand years old. Signs to the trail that once led to the Quinault tree have been removed. There are, however, still several Very Large Trees in the area, including the Big Sitka, one of our stops ahead. (For more information: www.quinaultrainforest.com/pages/giants.html; map is outdated and does not reflect the fall of the Western Red Cedar.)

2. Beach 4

Highway 101
About milepost 160.4
Map coordinates: 47.651361, -124.386864

Be aware that the trail down to Beach 4 is steeper than most in this book, with many stairs, and may be a bit much for some.

The coastline is dotted with little pocket beaches from north to south. What makes Beach 4 special (since obviously it's not its uninspired name; also called Kalaloch Beach 4) is its geology. At Beach 4, you can see some superior examples of the geological phenomenon known as "folded rocks"—that is, layers of rocks that have been bent or curved. Those who know what they're looking for will be able to see in places where the layers have been completely turned upside down. Regardless of your level of geological expertise, the rock formations are beautiful. What's more, this beach is less-visited than Ruby Beach, and the parking lot usually has plenty of room.

It is possible to walk north to Ruby Beach from here, but don't attempt it if you are not very aware of the timing of the tides and all other variables. You could easily get trapped with the tide rolling in, and that would not be good!

3. Tree Root Cave

Highway 101
Access from Kalaloch Campground parking lot
About milepost 157.6
Map coordinates: 47.612904, -124.374583

This tree is easy to get to—and easy to drive right by if you don't know it's there.

Drive into the Kalaloch Campground parking lot, follow the stairs and trail down to the beach, then head north (right). After a short walk (less than a hundred yards, maybe), the tree will be on your right.

Here, at the edge of the beach near the Kalaloch Campground, the iconic "Tree of Life," a Sitka spruce, clings to life at the edge of a cliff. The "Tree Root Cave" lies below it. The cave was caused by a small stream that ran/runs under the tree, eroding the soil under the roots over decades and forming a wide open space where the tree's supporting structure should be.

The tree makes for a dramatic sight. Some view this tree as a miracle, or as a symbol for resilience. To me, it represents tenacity, determination, and the importance of being able to adapt to life's challenges and changes. What's more, it's a metaphor for the fact that we all have at best a tenuous hold on life, and nothing lasts forever. If you're going to live your life, live it now. If you're going to see this tree before it collapses to the earth, go see it now.

And when you're there, be careful and considerate! This tree will fall one day, and that day could be one day soon. Don't be the one to make that happen. Hanging from the roots is not smart. Either you're contributing to the eventual demise, or you could find yourself in and amongst the ruins when it happens.

From here, head back toward Lake Quinault.

Optional Side Trip:

Kestner-Higley Homestead and Kestner Homestead Trail: This Homestead is on the N Shore Rd of Lake Quinault, whereas the other stops below are on the S Shore Rd. I would have put this on the main itinerary if the trip weren't already so long. The homestead and hike are doable in the same day as the rest of this trip (if you have some stamina), and are worth a visit for a lovely and interesting hike. The Kestner-Higley Homestead was once the homestead of, you guessed it, the Kestner and Higley families, who lived there from the late 1890s for several decades. There's an easy 1.3-mile hike through the homestead area, from which you can ponder the life of the rainforest pioneers, and which connects to a very short Maple Glade Nature Loop Trail. The homestead trailhead is next to the Quinault Rain Forest Ranger Station.

4. Merriman Falls

About 6.8 miles out S Shore Rd (after exiting Highway 101)
S Shore Rd, Quinault, WA 98575
Map coordinates: 47.500741, -123.784600

Drive back down Highway 101 and follow the signs toward S Shore Rd, Lake Quinault Lodge, and/or the Quinault Ranger Station (technically, the Pacific Ranger District - Quinault Office).

The next few stops take us out the S Shore Rd of Lake Quinault, and then backtrack to Highway 101 and home.

Merriman Falls is a gorgeous falls literally right next to the road. It has a fairy-like quality to it, with access to the falls from either side of the bridge. There's no signage to let you know it's coming up, but keep your eyes open for the bridge over Merriman Creek after the Colonel Bob Trailhead. The falls are on the right. Park on either side of the bridge.

Lack of rainfall makes this waterfall less spectacular in the fall, but it's still a lovely stop.

While you're out this way, keep your eyes open for elk. I once had to stop for several minutes as a whole herd crossed the road!

5. Big Spruce Tree (Largest Sitka Spruce Tree in the World)

S Shore Rd, Quinault, WA 98575
Map coordinates: 47.475788, -123.830530

Turn the car around to head west again on S Shore Rd, and drive back about 3.3 miles (if you hit the Post Office, you've gone just a bit too far). As you head west, the parking area for the Big Spruce Trail is on the left (south) side of the road; the trail itself is on the right (north). Park, cross carefully, and make the easy 0.2-mile walk to the Big Spruce Tree, the Largest Sitka Spruce Tree in the World. (As you cross a wooden bridge, the tree you're looking for is the one ahead of you and slightly to the right.) Signage at the tree gives the tree's measurements.

Optional Side Trip:
Gatton Creek Falls: If you can't get enough waterfalls, here's another: Travel 0.6 miles west on S Shore Rd from the Big Spruce, to the Gatton Creek Campground. Across the street from the Campground is a dirt road; head south-southeast on National Forest Local Road 160 / Wright's Canyon Rd for 0.4 miles. Park, and walk about 0.25 miles to the bridge and falls.

6. Falls Creek Falls

S Shore Rd, Quinault, WA 98575
Map coordinates: 47.468303, -123.845936

More waterfalls? Okay! Drive west on S Shore Rd 9.3 miles from the Big Spruce Trailhead (or 5.4 miles from Gatton Creek Campground, if you stopped at Gatton Creek Falls, too). To the south (left) is Quinault Mercantile; a bit farther down on the north (right) side of the street is the Ranger Station—a great place to stop in for a trail map, if you don't have one already. Park near the Mercantile. Falls Creek Falls runs under the bridge you just crossed; to get to it, zigzag on the Falls Creek Falls trail down to a great viewpoint.

7. Quinault Trail

S Shore Rd, Quinault, WA 98575
Map coordinates: 47.468303, -123.845936

But wait! We're not done! The trail you were just on actually continues on the other side of the road, as the Quinault Trail (or the Lodge Trail to Cascade Falls Loop, or Falls Creek Loop). This loop trail crosses Falls and Cascade Creeks and gives you a quintessential, yet fairly easy, rainforest hike experience. The 1.3-mile loop takes you on a walk among ancient spruce, maple, and cedar trees, by mosses and ferns, past creeks and waterfalls.

The trail ends back at S Shore Rd, across the street from Lake Quinault Lodge and about 0.15 miles west of where you started. Before heading back to your car, it's time to check out the area's famous Lodge!

8. Lake Quinault Lodge

345 S Shore Rd
Quinault, WA 98575
(360) 288-2900
www.olympicnationalparks.com/lodging/lake-quinault-lodge

This grand lodge is edging up on its 100-year anniversary, having been built in 1926. It's the kind of lodge you think of when you think of a lodge: rustic, warm, charming and inviting. The main lodge, with its grand fireplace and expansive view of Lake Quinault, is open to all. A bit of history, from the Lodge's website: "In the fall of 1937, President Franklin D. Roosevelt visited Lake Quinault Lodge during a fact-finding trip and enjoyed lunch in the later-named Roosevelt Dining Room. Nine months later, Roosevelt signed a bill creating Olympic National Park."

Check your watch at this point. Regardless of how much time you've spent at each spot, it's been a long day. If you head back now, you might hit a lot of traffic. Therefore, as I see it, you have two choices at this point:

1. Head home now and brave the evening commute traffic for 60 miles from Olympia all the way up to Seattle; or
2. Stop at the Lodge's bar or the Roosevelt Dining Room and have a drink and/or snack.

A warning: depending on how busy the lodge is, the bar may not always be open when it says it will be (starting at 3). The dining room opens at 5, year-round.

To get home, return to Highway 101 and retrace your route back to Seattle.

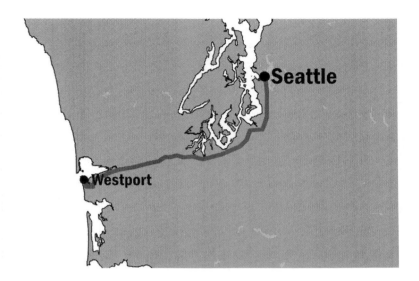

Stops:

1. Westport Winery
   (officially "Westport Winery Garden Resort")
2. Grays Harbor Lighthouse
3. Westport Observation Tower
   (also known as Westport Viewing Tower)
4. Westhaven State Park
5. Westport Light State Park

Westport

If a day at the beach is calling your name, pack a picnic, some beach chairs, and your sunscreen, and head west! And pack a blanket, too. Even in summer, the coast can have a chill.

Total miles driven: 360
Left home: 7:40 a.m.
Returned home: 7:40 p.m.

As with any trip to the beach, your main goal will be the sun (if you're lucky), the sand, the dunes, the call of the waves. This trip takes you to a winery with gorgeous gardens and a cute store, then to the state's tallest lighthouse, and then leaves room for plenty of time to become one with the beach.

Westport is about four miles south of the very popular Ocean Shores, but there's a bay in the way so to get from one to the other you have to go around the bay, which is about a 46-mile trip. Popular Ocean Shores can be overcrowded. Westport, in comparison, feels refreshing, clean, and open.

Like most ocean towns, Westport is wonderful for kite flying, surfing, gift shopping and antiquing, walking and hiking, beach-combing, getting some peace and quiet, and forgetting the troubles of the world.

Passes required:

A Discover Pass is required for the state parks. If you don't have one, you can buy one at the entrance to Westhaven State Park. More info at www.discoverpass.wa.gov.

Important notes:

Opening hours: If you want to actually go into the Grays Harbor Lighthouse, check before you go whether it'll be open when you're there. It's run by volunteers and as such has more limited hours than it might otherwise. www.westportmaritimemuseum.com/pricing-hours.

Shoes: If you plan to climb to the top of the lighthouse, don't wear sandals. The website doesn't list this restriction, but I've seen other reports that say they're not allowed.

Getting there:

Head south on I-5 to Highway 101, then west toward Aberdeen on WA State Route 8 west / US 12 west, then SR 105 south to the winery.

Stops:

1. Westport Winery
   (officially "Westport Winery Garden Resort")
2. Grays Harbor Lighthouse
3. Westport Observation Tower
   (also known as Westport Viewing Tower)
4. Westhaven State Park
5. Westport Light State Park

Optional Side Trip:

Tokeland Hotel & Restaurant: If you want to take this side trip, you'll need to go on the weekend, and you'll likely want to go first thing on your trip, as the restaurant is only open from 8 a.m. to 2 p.m. on Saturdays and Sundays. This hotel is considered by some to be haunted by "Charlie," a Chinese immigrant from the 1930s. Word is, he hid behind a fireplace and accidentally suffocated, and now haunts the building. Some say he sometimes tosses dinner plates around in the restaurant, so if you go, keep an eye on yours! Room 7 is the "most haunted," and there's also a ghost cat … they say. 100 Hotel Rd, Tokeland, WA 98590; www.tokelandhotel.com.

1. Westport Winery (officially "Westport Winery Garden Resort")

1 South Arbor Road
Aberdeen, WA 98520
www.westportwinery.com
(360) 648-2224
Fee: $5 for five tastes; fee is waived with each bottle purchase.

As you drive toward the winery, keep your eyes open: the turn into the winery parking lot comes up very quickly after a long stand of trees on the right (north). The winery's majestic 40-foot-tall lighthouse (which mimics, but is not an exact replica of, the Grays Harbor Lighthouse) will let you know you have arrived—and will also offer up your first photo op of many.

Westport Winery Garden Resort, which was ranked #1 in Evening Magazine's "Best of Western Washington" viewer poll in 2015, is more than just a winery. The owners have a stated goal: they want to become the Butchart Gardens of Washington state. (If you're not familiar with the Butchart Gardens, they are world-famous floral gardens near Victoria, B.C., and have been designated a National Historic Site of Canada.) While the winery will have to do some work to catch up, they are well on their way. You'll want to leave plenty of time to meander amongst the various gardens. Not only are the flowers and shrubs and grasses spectacular, but you'll also find whimsical art and stunning displays awaiting at every turn. Outdoor sculptures, commissioned by local artists, are interspersed throughout the fields of green and blooms. On our trip we discovered a giant sun, statues reminiscent of Easter Island, a mailbox draped in buoys, a bit of wood carved to look like an octopus, a shrub trimmed to the shape of a dolphin, and so much more.

And, of course, don't forget the wine! Inside you can taste five wines for $5. Your challenge will be how to pick just five from their very extensive list of choices. Many of the wines keep up the beach theme in their names: Lighthouse, Dawn Patrol, Charterboat Chick, Message in a Bottle, and Shorebird, just to name a few. They range from your standard reds and whites to some seductive blends and fruit and berry wines (Sweet Red Chocolate Blend, Sparkling Blueberry Pomegranate Muscat, Pineapple Riesling, and many more).

One note: a portion of the proceeds from every bottle of wine sold goes to a charity, amounting to thousands of dollars every year. The charity for each wine is listed on the wine list, so if you want to buy lots of bottles you can feel justified by knowing you are being quite charitable. The charities range from things like the local Audubon society, to the Aberdeen Museum of History, to the Grays Harbor Symphony, to PAWS, and so on. After all, there are more than three dozen wines, and each one gets its own charity! A very nice touch.

On your way out, check out the tiny store, which has a variety of gourmet foods as you'd expect, things like specialty jams and pickled vegetables and other gift items.

2. Grays Harbor Lighthouse

1020 W Ocean Ave
Westport, WA 98595
www.westportmaritimemuseum.com
Fee: From free up to $5 depending on age, military status, and more.

Grays Harbor Lighthouse is at the edge of the Westport Light State Park.

The first thing you might notice on arriving at the Grays Harbor Lighthouse is that it's ... well, it's in the middle of a forest. This may seem like an unlikely and perhaps even pointless positioning of a lighthouse, even for the tallest lighthouse in Washington (which this one is, standing 107 feet tall). What is it doing in a forest? As it turns out, in the 120 years since the lighthouse (also known as Westport Light) was built, the ocean has moved. Construction of jetties at the mouth of the harbor in the early 1900s changed the movement of sand and caused the ocean to essentially pull back; as a result, the lighthouse, which was originally about 300 feet from the shore, is now more than half a mile from the high tide mark.

Pro tip: the lighthouse is volunteer-run, and therefore is not open full time. In summer it's only open Friday through Monday (more closures the rest of the year). Be sure to check before you go whether it'll be open! If you do go when it's open, head inside to climb the 135 steps to the top for an expansive view of the area (and the surrounding trees). Entrance fee applies.

3. Westport Observation Tower

Westhaven Dr
Westport, WA 98595
Map coordinates: 46.911535, -124.117413

This observation tower is at the intersection of Cove Ave and Westhaven Dr, just before Westhaven Dr turns and becomes Neddie Rose Dr; at the very northern tip of Westport. There are a few parking spots at the very end of Westhaven Dr on the tower side of the road as it turns into Neddie Rose Dr.

Towers are for climbing, and this one's easy, with just fifty steps to the top. (If you use the ramp at the base of the tower, you can eliminate ten of those steps.) From the top of the tower you'll get lovely views out over Half Moon Bay and the Olympic Mountains if the day is clear, as well as the marina and downtown Westport. It's a great place to watch surfers or, if the timing is right, the sunset.

There are coin-operated binoculars at the top as well.

From the tower you may notice a paved trail. This is the Westport Light Trail. From the base of the tower, the trail more or less parallels the shoreline south for a bit and then west into Westhaven State Park to the parking lot, where it crosses Jetty Haul Road, skirts the edge of the parking lot, and then continues to track along the shoreline all the way down to Westport Light State Park (which is down by the lighthouse). The easy, kid-friendly, accessible trail from the Observation Tower to the Westport Light State Park parking lot is just about 2.3 miles, one way. There are limited easy beach access points along the way, as well as some bird-watching opportunities, and benches from which to watch the birds and the kite flyers and the waves and the world. The path generally lies a bit back from the shoreline and is ADA-accessible.

At the base of the tower are some picnic tables if you wanted to bring a lunch.

Optional Side Trip:
Maritime Museum: At this point, you're close to the Westport Maritime Museum (2201 Westhaven Dr, Westport, WA 98595). Where else will you find exhibits on knot tying and beachcombing?

4. Westhaven State Park

2700 Jetty Haul Rd
Westport, WA 98595
Map coordinates: 46.902041, -124.128613
Discover Pass required

Westhaven State Park is, as the name suggests, a State Park, and therefore requires a Discover Pass. If you don't already have one, you're in luck; there's a handy kiosk at the entrance at which you can buy either a Day Pass or an Annual Pass (a much better deal, if you're into day trips!).

The thing about dunes is they tend to hide treasures. You see a great hill, but you can't see much of what's beyond. This is the case here, as well. A peek over the dunes at Westhaven State Park is well worth your time.

Climb up and over the dunes, and lo and behold, a vast beach lies before you. It's so perfect I almost hesitate to tell you about it, but now you know. Bring your book, your blanket, your beach chair, your bucket and beachcombing eyes, your picnic, whatever it is you like to have with you for a day at the beach, and you're set for hours.

For bonus points, clean up after not only yourself, but pick up a few pieces of someone else's trash as well.

There are clean restrooms by the parking lot.

5. Westport Light State Park

1595 Ocean Ave
Westport, WA 98595
Map coordinates: 46.886789, -124.123732
parks.state.wa.us/284/Westport-Light
Discover Pass required

Westhaven State Park and Westport Light State Park seem to blend together, but are, in fact, two separate parks. Westhaven State Park is at the northwest end of the peninsula, and Westport Light State Park is a bit south of it; Grays Harbor Lighthouse is at the very southeast edge of Westport Light State Park.

To complete your Westport experience, drive around to Westport Light State Park for a view of the beach from a different angle. All trails leaving from the parking lot eventually end up at the Westport Light Trail, also known as the "Dunes Trail," and discussed above in the description of the Westport Observation Tower.

When you've had enough of the rest and relaxation, the sun and sand, the seagulls and seashells, head on home.

Optional Side Trip:

Polson Museum: This National Historic Site, built in 1924, is another spot you have to time right, or you'll miss it. Open Wednesday through Saturday 11 to 4, Sundays 12 to 4. The Polson family lived in this mansion with its twenty-six rooms, six bathrooms, and four fireplaces, until 1965, when they moved to Seattle. Now it is a museum, painstakingly restored over three decades. The grounds include gardens and displays of outdoor machinery; inside are various exhibits with photographs, artifacts, and antiques documenting the history of the family, the house, and the Grays Harbor area. 1611 Riverside Avenue, Hoquiam, WA 98550; www. polsonmuseum.org.

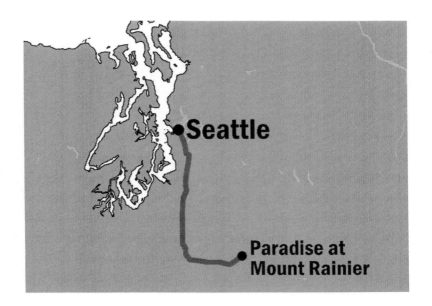

Stops:

1. Christine Falls
2. Paradise Visitor Center
3. Myrtle Falls
4. Reflection Lake
5. Box Canyon (part of the Wonderland Trail)
6. Picnic view at Backbone Ridge View Point
7. Grove of the Patriarchs

Mount Rainier / Paradise

With almost two million visitors annually, Mount Rainier National Park is one of the state's most-visited attractions. It is America's fifth oldest national park, established in 1899.

Total miles driven: 255
Left home: 8:00 a.m.
Returned home: 6:00 p.m.

Mount Rainier is one of those iconic Seattle things in which locals forget to partake. After all, it's always there. It's not going anywhere. It's been there for 500,000 years (yes, I looked that up), and it will likely be there another for another 500,000 years. Or, at least, it will be around longer than you and I will be around. So we admire it from afar; we gasp at it as we drive down I-5; but we forget to visit. But this mountain is not just iconic and gorgeous; it's definitely worth a visit. Or ten.

Assuming you're probably taking this trip in the summer, the earlier you can leave, the better, especially if you want to spend time at Paradise or other popular spots.

The mountain itself is, in my opinion, one of the planet's most spectacular mountains. It stands at 14,410 feet high, majestic and snow-capped and awe-inspiring, and the fifth highest peak (and tallest volcano) in the contiguous US. If you're in the area and you hear someone say, "the mountain is out!" You might wonder what that means until you realize that on many days, cloudy or hazy skies keep Rainier hidden from sight. When the mountain is out, it is breathtaking. Still after all these years, the sight of this dormant (technically, "episodically active") volcano against a crisp blue sky will literally make me gasp. I admit it, I'm a little bit in love with this mountain.

Admittedly, depending on your starting point, a trip to Mount Rainier can make for a very long day. Plus, it's not like the mountain is going anywhere; looming large and magnificent on the horizon, it's always there, waiting for you. Before I started this book, I can't even tell you how many years it had been since I'd made the trek. But it's worth it.

With nearly 370 square miles of land within its boundaries, obviously there's more than one day's worth to explore. Countless hiking books and websites are devoted to its trails, so I won't try to be any sort of authority or comprehensive listing. Instead, what I'm offering here is simply one possible trip you could take. Do some research in those hiking books and park websites to find more trails and areas that appeal to your own desires.

Passes required:

Getting into the park is not cheap, but it's worth it! If you plan to go more than once or to other National lands, you can cut the expenses by getting something other than a day pass. The annual America the Beautiful pass (www.nps.gov/planyourvisit/passes.htm) works and is a great choice; other options are listed at the Mount Rainier website (www.nps.gov/mora/planyourvisit/fees.htm).

Important notes:

Timing: Due to snow (it is a mountain, after all), not all areas are open at all times. Check the website before you go. www.nps.gov/mora/planyourvisit/basicinfo.htm.

Gas: No gas stations within the park. Make sure you're gassed up before you enter.

Food: You can eat lunch at a handful of restaurants or snack bars inside the park, but your food options are limited. Pack a picnic and stay a while! If you're planning to hike, be sure to bring lots of water. One guideline is to drink one liter of water per two hours. Your mileage may vary. Plan accordingly.

Danger: If you're hiking, be cognizant that there are inherent dangers involved. At least four hundred people have died on Mount Rainier since 1897 (mostly on longer treks, but not all). Take the 10 essentials and be smart. www.wta.org/go-outside/basics/ten-essentials.

Cell phone / internet: Once you're in the park you won't be connected, so be prepared. Take a map.

Getting there:

Many roads lead to Paradise. One option is to take I-5 South to Exit 127. Take Exit 127. Follow your GPS as you take WA 512 E, then WA 704 E, then WA 7 S, then eventually WA 706 E, and on into Paradise. You'll need to stop at the entrance kiosk to show your pass before you can get into the park.

Stops:

1. Christine Falls
2. Paradise Visitor Center
3. Myrtle Falls
4. Reflection Lake
5. Box Canyon (part of the Wonderland Trail)
6. Picnic view at Backbone Ridge View Point
7. Grove of the Patriarchs

Optional Side Trips:

The first Visitor Center: Within the park but before Christine Falls, the first stop on this itinerary, you'll see signs for Longmire (www.visitrainier.com/places-and-attractions/park-regions/longmire). Longmire was Mount Rainier's first Visitor Center, back when the park was established in 1899. Before that, it was James Longmire's homestead.

Wildflowers: The Mount Rainier area was once voted "Best Wildflower Spot in The United States." If you want a wildflower hike, Visit Rainier has made it easy for you, compiling their Top 10 Wildflower Hikes: www.visitrainier.com/wildflowers.

1. Christine Falls

Map coordinates: 46.780822, -121.779475

www.visitrainier.com/christine-falls

Two-tiered Christine Falls can be seen from either side of Paradise Valley Road. Parking is available both before and after the bridge. A short walk from the parking area after the bridge will take you to a viewpoint from which many a photographer has taken a photo of the falls and the picturesque bridge.

Whether you see this as a great photo opportunity or a chance to gaze in wonder at one of the park's most spectacular falls, this is well worth a stop. When I last visited, a woman from Wisconsin was there at the same time. Her eyes wide with wonder, locked on the sight before her, she said to me, "We don't have anything like this!"

Optional Side Trip:

Comet Falls Trail: Just before Christine Falls, you'll pass the trailhead for Comet Falls. If you look up from the bridge at Christine Falls, in fact, you'll see part of the Comet Falls trail. This 3.8-mile (round trip) moderate hike will take you past myriad small falls as well as the namesake Comet Falls and the beautiful Christine Falls. At more than 300 feet, Comet Falls is one of the highest falls in the park. Parking at the trailhead is very limited. www.visitrainier.com/van-trump-park-comet-falls.

2. Paradise Visitor Center

(Henry M Jackson Memorial Visitor Center at Paradise)
Map coordinates: 46.785540, -121.736757
www.visitrainier.com/henry-m-jackson-memorial-visitor-center-at-paradise

If you want to see a crowded parking lot (with amazing scenery), head to Paradise Visitor Center in the summer. It's possible you may not find one, so be prepared to either circle the lot, or move on.

Paradise is the most popular destination in Mount Rainier National Park. Around 60 to 65 percent of visitors to the park head to Paradise each year. If you figure 2 million visitors in a year (the most recent number I found was 1.86 million in 2015), 60 to 65 percent of 2 million is 1.2 to 1.3 million visitors to Paradise each year. Divide that by 365 days and you have 3200 to 3500 visitors every day. And of course the visits are not spread out evenly though the year; in winter, the number will be far less, and in summer, far more. We went on a Wednesday in July, and at 10:30 a.m. the parking lot at Paradise was already past overflowing.

The good thing is, there's no shortage of trails and viewpoints outside of Paradise. Even if you don't get to spend time at Paradise, I doubt you'll leave the park disappointed.

If you do score a parking spot, take some time to wander around this spectacular view point, then head to the Visitor Center to pick up a map, find out about the numerous trails in the area, and ask any questions you might have. Restrooms are available outside the Visitor Center.

The next stop on this itinerary, Myrtle Falls trail, leaves from the Paradise lot.

3. Myrtle Falls

www.visitrainier.com/myrtle-falls

A very easy hike for a fantastic reward. From the Visitor Center or behind Paradise Inn, follow signs to the Skyline Trail. Myrtle Falls will be a little less than a half mile along the trail. This is one of the most photographed areas of the park, so likely you'll encounter many fellow photographers.

4. Reflection Lake

Map coordinates: 46.768529, -121.731748
www.visitrainier.com/reflection-lakes-2

A quick image search on the internet will reveal tons of magnificent and coveted mirror photos of Mount Rainier reflected in the aptly named Reflection Lake. The good news: the lake is right next to the road, so you hardly have to walk at all to get a great shot. The bad news (unless you're a real morning person): the reflection will be best in the wee hours of the morning, when the water is still calm. Later in the day, there may be no reflection at all. You might try your luck again at sunset, when waters have quieted again. Whenever you visit, it's a beautiful site to take a deep breath and to stretch your legs.

Optional Side Trip:
Reflection Lakes Trail: You don't have to hike to enjoy this lake, but you can if you want to. The Reflection Lakes trail is a moderate, 2.75-mile loop from which you can experience the wonders

of the mountain and the passing seasons: wildflowers in summer, autumn colors in fall. Take a map and follow signs; the multitudes of connecting trails can get confusing.

5. Box Canyon (part of the Wonderland Trail)

Map coordinates: 46.765746, -121.634942
On Stevens Canyon Road, 12 miles (19.3k) west of the Ohanapecosh Visitor Center or 17.5 miles (28.2k) east of Longmire
www.visitrainier.com/wonderland-trail-pt-5-box-canyon-to-longmire

The Box Canyon Trail is part of / attached to the (very) much longer Wonderland Trail (a 93-mile-long trail that circles the whole mountain; a bit more than a day trip!). This very easy loop is about a half mile long. Park in the lot on the right side of the road and cross to the left side. Basically the trail itself is shaped like a box—up, over the bridge, and back—but a "box canyon" refers to a canyon which has a single entrance and exit, and is boxed in on the other sides. (From what I can tell, a box canyon is generally wider than a slot canyon, but they are much the same in many respects.) This particular canyon reaches depths of 180 feet, and is about 13 feet wide at its narrowest point.

From the bridge in the middle of the walk, or the bridge at the end of the walk (where the road is), look down and you'll see the water of the Muddy Fork Cowlitz River rushing by. Be sure to look down at the canyon from both sides of the road. Because the canyon is so narrow, which view is best will change a great deal depending on the time of day and the angle of the sun, so check it out from every viewpoint!

There are some great views of Mount Rainier at the beginning of the walk, too, (assuming you start on the right side and walk the trail counterclockwise) and at the right time of the year, a nice field of wildflowers.

Back at the parking lot, you can walk down to an overlook. You can't see the canyon terribly well from here, but you do get a good glimpse out at Mount Adams to the south, weather permitting.

6. Picnic view at Backbone Ridge View Point

Map coordinates: 46.710079, -121.600411
Along Stevens Canyon Road

Along the route between Box Canyon and Grove of the Patriarchs, there's a somewhat strange- and rather industrial-looking roadside pullout with picnic tables, almost as though the picnic tables were an afterthought. Regardless, pull over and have your picnic at this spot, because the views from here are breathtaking.

You might well encounter ravens in this area. If you see one, look around for another; ravens almost always mate for life, and are territorial; therefore, you'll often encounter two together, but rarely a crowd. A group of ravens, by the way, is an "unkindness" or "conspiracy," which hardly seems fair for such intelligent creatures!

7. Grove of the Patriarchs

Map coordinates: 46.758229, -121.557694
Stevens Canyon Road
www.visitrainier.com/grove-of-the-patriarchs-2

To hike this easy trail, you'll start by heading north on the Eastside Trail for about a third of a mile, then branch off to the right onto the Grove of the Patriarchs trail (a little less than a third of a mile). Cross over the Ohanapecosh River via a somewhat precarious suspension bridge; a sign on the trail suggests you limit yourself to one person on the bridge at a time. A boardwalk loop at the end of the Grove of the Patriarchs trail will immerse amongst giant old-growth Douglas firs, hemlocks, and cedars. Walking alongside some fallen trees on the trail can give you an even better sense of their enormity. Interpretive signage helps tell the stories of these ancient residents, some of which are more than a thousand years old.

The trail itself is fairly easy, and great for kids and families, but note that it is a bit uneven in places. When I went, on my way in I saw a stroller on the side of the trail that had been abandoned; on my way out, I noticed it had been reclaimed and was gone.

SR 123 is closed in winter. If it's closed, retrace your route and head home. If it's open, allow yourself some variety and follow 123 north to where it joins with 410; follow 410 north and west, and get your GPS to tell you how to get home from there.

Optional Side Trips:
Silver Falls Loop: Another popular trail in this area is the Silver Falls Loop (www.visitrainier.com/silver-falls) an easy 2.7-mile loop that features hot springs and waterfalls. The loop leaves from

the Ohanapecosh Visitors Center; for an even shorter hike, park on SR 123 across the street from the Three Lakes Trail on the east side, and follow the falls trail on the west side to the falls.

Up in the air: Shortly after SR 123 connects with 410, you'll pass Crystal Mountain. From the Crystal Mountain Resort, you can ride the eight-passenger Mount Rainier Gondola, a 10-minute adventure in the sky (www.visitrainier.com/ride-mt-rainier-gondola).

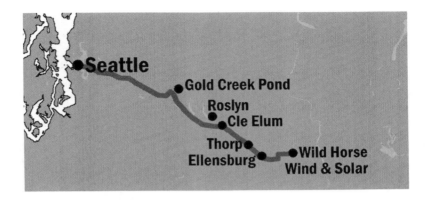

Stops:

1. Wild Horse Renewable Energy Center
2. Dick & Jane's Spot
3. Historic Downtown Ellensburg
4. Thorp Fruit & Antique Mall
5. Downtown Cle Elum
6. The Brick & Pennsylvania Avenue in Roslyn
7. Roslyn Cemetery
8. Cle Elum Lake / Speelyi Beach Park
9. Gold Creek Pond Trail

Ellensburg, Cle Elum, and Roslyn

This day trip offers up a Central Cascades sampler; a smorgasbord of sites, if you will. From a vision of the future at a wind farm, to many trips into the past, Ellensburg, Cle Elem, and Roslyn have it all.

Total miles driven: 316
Left home: 7:15 a.m.
Returned home: 6:15 p.m.

This is the second-longest trip in the book. Skipping the Wild Horse Renewable Energy Center will save you time and miles, but it's interesting and worth a visit once (if only to dispel the idea that windmills kill lots of birds).

Passes required:

A Northwest Forest Pass or Interagency Annual Pass (America the Beautiful Pass) is needed for Gold Creek Pond Trail.

Important notes:

Timing: If you want to take the 10 a.m. tour at the Wild Horse Renewable Energy Center, the challenge, of course, is getting your departure time right. I left at 7:15 a.m., thinking that would give me plenty of time. No surprise, then, that I got stopped behind an accident on I-5. I reached the facility at about 10:03. They ask you to be there 10 minutes early, so technically I was about 15 minutes late, but no one else was there yet. Very soon after I got there, another eight people showed up. Tour departure time is somewhat flexible, then, but I'd still recommend leaving no later than about 7 a.m.

Clothes: If you take the wind farm tour, you'll be required to wear closed-toed shoes.

Getting there:

To begin, head east on I-90. Follow directions to the Wild Horse Renewable Energy Center (NOT the Wild Horse Wind & Solar Facility, which is on the way, but which is not your final destination).

Stops:

1. Wild Horse Renewable Energy Center
2. Dick & Jane's Spot
3. Historic Downtown Ellensburg
4. Thorp Fruit & Antique Mall
5. Downtown Cle Elum
6. The Brick & Pennsylvania Avenue in Roslyn
7. Roslyn Cemetery
8. Cle Elum Lake / Speelyi Beach Park
9. Gold Creek Pond Trail

1. Wild Horse Renewable Energy Center

25905 Vantage Hwy
Ellensburg, WA 98926
509) 964-7815
www.pse.com/inyourcommunity/ToursandRecreation/WildHorse/
Pages/default.aspx

Guided tours at 10 a.m. and 2 p.m. (weather permitting)
Open April 1-Nov. 15, 9:00 a.m. to 5:00 p.m.
Closed Nov. 16-March 31

Note: shortly after you turn off of the Vantage Highway onto Beacon Ridge Road, there's a building on the left. This is NOT your destination. This is the Wild Horse Wind & Solar Facility. What you want is the Wild Horse Renewable Energy Center (basically the visitor center), a little more than three miles farther along the road. Keep driving!

Driving along I-90, or many other places in the world, you've likely seen the modern day windmills in the hills: towering wind turbines, pointing 221 feet into the sky, each with its three 129-foot-long blades cutting through the air. (And weighing 257 tons each! That's 514,000 pounds!) But how much do you know about wind farms? Stop in for a free tour to find out how wind farms have changed since the 1980s—most notably, if you have it in your head that wind farms kill lots of birds, that's old news. Learn all about it in an information-packed tour led by a knowledgable intern. Tours last about an hour, and you'll walk about 1/3 mile. You do have to sign a liability form and wear a hard hat and safety goggles. If, like me, you don't love the idea of wearing hats that other people have worn, rest assured: they disinfect the hats after every wearing.

Also note: If you haven't worn closed-toed shoes and want to go on the tour, they will make you put on a pair of Crocs they provide.

Puget Sound Energy, who designed and run this visitor center, have done a great job. The exhibits are informative and interesting, and the staff are friendly and full of facts. What's more, the daily tours aren't your only chance to explore the area and facility. Check out their website for events from April through November, including wildflower and wind power walks, a hike through the Ponderosa Pines, kids' activities, Run Like the Wind races, a Perseid star party, Hunter's breakfast, a Wild Horse Behind the Scenes tour, and more.

If you miss the 10 a.m. or 2 p.m. tours, you can still explore the main visitor center and walk around on the grounds to an extent. Watch out for snakes! (Really!) And cows! (Really!)

2. Dick & Jane's Spot

101 N Pearl St
Ellensburg, WA 98926
www.reflectorart.com/spot

This home-made labor of love and art has been in constant construction and collection for forty years, and now is home to the works of more than forty Northwest artists. A visual cornucopia to brighten your heart, the artwork at Dick and Jane's house bursts with color and whimsy. Jane Orleman and her late husband Dick Elliott have compiled and created sculptures, carvings, a reflector fence, bottle cap art, and much more. You're almost certain to walk away with a lighter step.

Find a place to park—but not in front of the house, which must be clear to accommodate fire trucks! Stroll the perimeter of the artful home, minding the fences and the fact that it's a private residence. You can't go in (unless you're invited by the owners, obviously), but there's enough to see from the outside to put plenty of smiles on your face.

The Culture Trip included Dick & Jane's Spot in their 2017 list, "The Top 10 Things Every Washington Art Lover Should Experience."

3. Historic Downtown Ellensburg

Water Street to Ruby Street; 2nd Ave to 6th Ave
Ellensburg, WA 98926

Historic Downtown Ellensburg is a more-or-less four-square-block area, roughly bounded to the west by Water Street; to the east by Ruby Street; to the south by 2nd Ave; and to the north by 6th Ave. Dick & Jane's Spot is just a block away, so your parking spot will have you in easy walking distance. Wander the streets and discover book stores, craft beer, art galleries, cafes and taverns, gift stores, museums, wineries, parks, and more.

Tip: If you're getting hungry by now, grab a snack, but I recommend you save a good bit of room for a meal at The Brick in Roslyn!

4. Thorp Fruit & Antique Mall

220 Gladmar Rd
Thorp, WA 98946
(509) 964-2474
www.thorpfruit.com

If you've driven out I-90, chances are you've seen Thorp Fruit &
Antique Mall. The signage on the building is enormous: you truly
can't miss it. But if you haven't stopped before, now's the time.

The Thorp Fruit & Antique Mall started in 1944 as a simple
fruit stand, and has grown today into a thriving third-generation
business. Upstairs is an antique mall with a plethora of collectibles,
antiques, and vintage items. Downstairs the store carries fresh seasonal produce, and gourmet specialty grocery items year-round.
What kind of variety do they have? Well, on the day I was last
there, this was just a sampling: dry soup and cake mixes, honey ha-
banero barbecue sauce, saltwater taffy, Kalamata olive bread sticks,
jalapeño bagels, mango white balsamic vinegar, maple bacon onion jam, lemon curd, bourbon honey, tons of wines, Walla Walla
sweet onion mustard with chipotle, butternut squash pasta sauce,
Sriracha aioli, sweet potato butter, raspberry pepper jelly, jalapeño
pickled asparagus, sauerkraut salad, and much, much, much more!
Stop in and treat yourself to something delicious.

Optional Side Trip:
Historic Thorp Mill: According to their website, "the Thorp Grist
Mill is the only remaining mill in Washington state that made the
transition from stone buhr to modern rollers." It is now open to
visitors, for self-guided tours year-round, and guided tours May
through August. Limited hours, so check before you go! 11640 N.
Thorp Hwy, Thorp, WA 98946, www.thorp.org.

5. Downtown Cle Elum

Map coordinates: 47.196108, -120.940228

I'll be honest: Cle Elem can be a challenge, in that it feels like nothing is ever open. I've driven by the Telephone Museum a million times when it's been closed. The other day I drove by the Carpenter House Museum: closed. As is the case with many businesses in small towns, being open every day, all day, is simply not a sustainable business model. Still, it's a town worth a stroll. Wander a bit and see what's open!

Cle Elum Telephone Museum
221 East First Street
Cle Elum, WA 98922
Open May thru Sept 12 p.m. to 4 p.m.
Oldest complete telephone museum west of the Mississippi. Free admission.

Carpenter Family Historic Home & Art Gallery
302 West Third St.
Cle Elum WA 98922
509-674-2313
kittitashistory.com/sites/carpenter-house/
Open Friday through Sunday, noon to 4 p.m.
The Carpenter in this case is not a builder, but rather Carpenter was the family name of Cle Elum's first successful banker. This 1914 mansion is believed to be a "pattern book" house—that is, one where a person would pick a pattern of a home from a catalog, and you'd be sent a set of blueprints and a list of all the building materials you would need to build the home. Inside the home now,

one can step back into time to experience the story of the Carpenter family.

Check the Cle Elum calendar of events (www.discovercleelum. com/events) to see what else might be going on while you're in town.

Optional Side Trip:
Historic Coal Mines Trail: If you want to hike a longer trail, the Coal Mines Trail is just under 5 miles each way. This gentle trail (suitable for walking, running, hiking, horseback riding, and biking) leads from Cle Elum along Crystal Creek through Roslyn and up to Ronald, past a variety of historic coal mining sites and remains. The trail began life as a railway bed for Northern Pacific Railroad in 1886, transporting coal and residents, and closed one hundred years later. In 1994, work began to convert it to its present use. The trail is well maintained.

6. The Brick & Pennsylvania Avenue in Roslyn

100 W Pennsylvania Ave
Roslyn WA 98941
www.bricksaloon.com

Are you hungry yet? Now is your chance. Stop at The Brick for a bite to eat and a bit of history. The Brick, established in 1889, lays claim to Washington's first business license as well as Washington's first liquor license—at least, that's what the very friendly and personable waiter told me. "Washington's oldest continuously operating bar," says their website; "From our famous 100 year old bar showcasing the original 23' running water spittoon, to our basement jail cell, colorful coal mining history, tasty pub fare, and live music every Friday and Saturday night, The Brick is sure to be your favorite roadhouse stop!"

Fans of the 1990–1995 TV show Northern Exposure might also recognize it as the bar and restaurant in fictitious Cicely, Alaska, owned and operated by Holling Vincoeur. The Brick also makes an appearance in the 1979 film The Runner Stumbles, starring Dick Van Dyke.

You might think that as it's been twenty-five years since Northern Exposure went off the air, the town would no longer be drawing fans of the show. If you thought that, however, you would be wrong. The waiter at The Brick told me that every day they still get fans in, coming from all over the country and the world. When I was there, I saw people in The Brick and all over Pennsylvania Avenue, taking pictures of themselves in front of iconic Northern Exposure signs.

After you've had your fill of The Brick's offerings, head down Pennsylvania Avenue to see these sites for yourself. (Be warned: viewing these sites may induce a desire to go back and re-watch the series!) Kitty corner from The Brick is the home of KBHR radio studio, where Chris Stevens would muse and wax poetic on the frailties and foibles of humanity. Back on The Brick's side of the street and down a couple buildings, the gift shop is named "Cicely's Gift Shop"; this building, which in the show was the office of Dr. Fleischman, still bears Dr. Joel Fleishman's name painted across the front window. Farther down the street, Northern Exposure fans will instantly recognize the moose mural at Roslyn Cafe. (In the show, they added a tiny 's to the name, making it Roslyn's Cafe. The cafe also serves great food.

P.S. My first series, the Wishing Rock series, have been called

"Northern Exposure-esque." If you loved the quirky residents and stories of Cicely, Alaska, give the Wishing Rock books a try! Start with *Letters from Wishing Rock (a novel with recipes)*.

7. Roslyn Cemetery

Memorial St
Cle Elum, WA 98922

Even if you're not into cemeteries, the Roslyn Cemetery is worth a visit. When you first drive up you might think the reasonable-sized cemetery on your left is your destination. Well, it is—and it isn't. The cemetery is actually more than two dozen different cemeteries (I've read 25 to 27; not sure which is correct), grouped by various ethnic, civil and fraternal organizations, and nestled all together in the woods. From Druids to Veterans to Foresters to Masonic Lodge to Eagles to Serbians and beyond, each lay their own to rest in a separate but adjacent cemetery. Take some time to wander amongst the various cemeteries and note the differences in the burial customs among the nearly five thousand graves.

8. Cle Elum Lake / Speelyi Beach Park

Lake Cabins Rd
Cle Elum, WA 98922

Remember in the intro when I talked about road trips being about discovery and the journey? This stop is purely about discovery: I'm taking you to Speelyi Beach Park simply because chances are you've probably never been there. (And also to give you a glimpse at Cle Elum Lake, which is lovely.) Off-road vehicles can drive down to the lake; otherwise, park in the small lot and walk down to the lake, maybe 100 yards or so from the parking area.

Supposedly there's another public access point farther up the Salmon La Sac Road, at Morgan Creek Campground. However, when I tried to find it I found what seems to now be a privately owned area. Has Morgan Creek Campground been sold off to a private owner? Or was I looking in the wrong place? If you find out for sure, let me know.

9. Gold Creek Pond Trail

Snoqualmie Pass, WA 98068
Map coordinates: 47.396541, -121.379373
www.wta.org/go-hiking/hikes/gold-creek-pond
Pass required: $5/day, or Northwest Forest Pass or America the Beautiful Interagency Pass. (Discover Pass is NOT valid here.)

I know, it's been a long day and you're tired and you just want to get home, but I implore you not to skip this stop. You might well find a new favorite place! Besides which, you want to avoid rush hour, don't you? Stop here and pass some time, and your commute home will be a breeze!

On a trip across the pass, it's easy to whip by Gold Creek Pond Trail without even knowing it exists. It's right by the summit of Snoqualmie Pass (and therefore, I'm guessing, inaccessible in winter). But this clear blue pond is worth a visit. You could well end up putting it on your list of places to return to; next time with a picnic!

Park in the lot and make sure your pass is visible on your car's dash. (As with most trailheads, it's wisest not to leave anything in your car, lest vandals see it and try to break in.) Walk 1/10 of a mile from the parking lot to where the loop trail will take you either left or right. Go left, and you'll soon hit an area with half a dozen picnic tables and heaps of serene beauty. The loop trail is almost exactly a mile long; add 2/10 of a mile for the track to and from the parking lot. The paved, ADA-accessible, interpretive trail is level and easy for almost everyone. Even with the hum of cars on I-90 not too far in the distance, this stop will bring you a drop of bliss.

Once you've had your fill of the peace and calm, head back to I-90, and on to home.

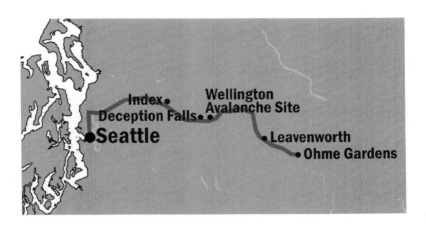

Stops:

1. Index
2. Wellington Avalanche Site
3. Ohme Gardens (past Leavenworth)
4. Leavenworth
5. Deception Falls

Leavenworth

Round out your trip to this well-known and ever-busy Bavarian town with a few hidden gems you'll want to return to again and again.

Total miles driven: 275
Left home: 8:00 a.m.
Returned home: 5:00 p.m.

Leavenworth is no secret, but you'll want to be sure to stick around to the end of this day trip! This book starts with my favorite day trip, Diablo Lake, and ends with my favorite little-known gem, Deception Falls, not to be confused with Deception Pass!

Passes required:

A Northwest Forest Pass or Interagency Annual Pass (America the Beautiful Pass) is needed for the Wellington site. If you need to buy one en route, there's a Ranger Station (USDA FS–Skykomish

Ranger District) on US 2 at 74920 Northeast Stevens Pass Highway Skykomish, WA 98288. This is about 10 miles before Deception Falls and about 15 miles before the turnoff that leads to Wellington.

Important notes:

Gas: Skykomish (just before Stevens Pass) will be your last chance to get gas before Leavenworth (about 50 miles away), so fill up!

Getting there:

Random Road Fact: Did you know that U.S. Route 2 takes you all the way from Everett, Washington, to St. Ignace, Michigan? And that there's a second segment of the road, starting in Rouses Point, New York and ending in Houlton, Maine? And, what's more, the Washington State Legislature defines the Washington portion of U.S. Route 2 as State Route 2?

This day trip takes you on the first part of the route, whether you refer to it as U.S. Route 2 or State Route 2 (or, as I've always thought of it, Highway 2). However you'd like to get there, find your way to U.S. Route 2 from Seattle, and head east.

Stops:

1. Index
2. Wellington Avalanche Site
3. Ohme Gardens (past Leavenworth)
4. Leavenworth
5. Deception Falls

NOTE: Since this is an out-and-back route, you can do these in whatever order you like. On the map, west to east, their order is: Index, Deception Falls, Wellington Avalanche Site, Leavenworth, Ohme Gardens.

1. Index

Map coordinates: 47.820107, -121.554247

As you're heading out U.S. Route 2, it's easy to miss the town of Index. For one thing, it's not immediately off the road. For another, with a population of just under 200 (as of 2016), it's small. Index is well known to rock climbers, and the people who live there, and … well, that's about it.

Any town along a river is worth a stop in my book, though, and this is my book, so we're making a stop here. From US 2, turn left onto Index-Galena Rd (watch for it shortly after the signs for Lake Serene and Bridal Veil Falls Trailhead), and follow the road into town.

As with all small towns, for economic necessity stores are open fewer hours. If they're open stop at The River House (444 Avenue A, Index, Washington, WA 98256) for a beer and a burger, or pop next door to the Outdoor Adventure Center to see what they have to offer, from river rafting and adventure tours, to rentals, and more.

Take a slow drive along the few roads, and stop at the intersection of 2nd St and Ave A. There's a bench there where you can sit a while, watch the Skykomish River rush by, take in the peace of the views, and enjoy the scenery.

If you start thinking about moving there, stay long enough to find out how often the trains go by! It's not infrequent.

Optional Side Trip:
Heybrook Lookout: The trailhead for this short (2.6-mile) and moderately steep hike is on US 2, shortly after Index, around mile marker 37. About 1.3 miles in, you'll reach the Heybrook Lookout. Climb the eighty-nine stairs to get a bird's-eye view of Mt. Baker-Snoqualmie National Forest and the valley.

2. Wellington Avalanche Site (also known as Wellington Ghost Town ... may be haunted??)

Map coordinates: 47.747536, -121.126547

Once back on US 2, follow it for about 28.5 miles. Watch on your left for Tye Road, also known as the Old Cascade Highway; turn left onto Tye Road. Follow this "rough but passable" road for 2.8 miles. At 2.8 miles, you'll see a road on the right. When I was there, it wasn't marked, but this is indeed the road you want. Turn right and follow the road the rest of the way to the Wellington Avalanche Site. (From experience, I can tell you that if you go too far, about two miles farther on the road dead-ends at what used to be a bridge over the Tye River. It's also scenic, but it's not what you're looking for!)

Little-known fact: an avalanche along Stevens Pass in 1910 was and remains the deadliest avalanche in U.S. History. Ninety-six lives were lost on March 1, 1910, at the Wellington town site, which has since been renamed Tye to try to distance it from the disaster. On that day, passengers and trainmen on a Great Northern Railway (also known as the Iron Goat) train encountered a massive ten-day snowstorm (what actually turned out to be three storms, one after the other) en route from Spokane to Seattle. With snow falling at the rate of a foot an hour, by the time they reached Wellington, the train had to stop, finding themselves "parked" next to a mail train that was also waiting for the storm to pass. They were stuck for nearly a week when the snow turned to driving rain, thunder and lightning. As everyone slept, at about 1:43 a.m. on March 1, a lightning strike broke the avalanche loose and nearly a hundred people died.

You can still see some of the remains of the town, including foundations, concrete snow sheds, the Cascade Tunnel, and a Vietnam-era tank. A kiosk in the parking area will point you to the various sites. These easy hiking trails are suitable for most levels of hiking ability.

For a great and detailed overview of the avalanche, the area, and what all you can see there, go to www.exploringhistoryinyourhikingboots.com/iron-goat-wellington-wa-usa. For a fantastic "guided tour" via YouTube by author, historian, and photographer Martin Burwash, see the video titled "Exploring the Remains of the Wellington Avalanche of 1910" at www.youtube.com/watch?v=RHTyu8Ecqyc (credit: TracksideNW), or the concurrently recorded video "Martin Burwash Tour of the 1910 Wellington Snow-Slide Disaster" at www.youtube.com/watch?v=wOzfUiz599w (credit: Joel Hawthorn). Martin Burwash also has written a book (somewhat fictionalized) on the topic: Vis Major: Railroad Men, an 'Act of God'—White Death at Wellington.

Some say the area is haunted, especially at the observation deck and the snow shed. If you have a sighting, let me know!

NOTE: Disruption of bear habitat in recent years, especially due to wildfires, has increased bear activity all over. Recently I read a report of a brown bear following someone in the snow shed. Be alert, and bring a friend!

Optional Side Trip:
Iron Goat Trail: If you want to add a trail to your day's mix, the Iron Goat Trail is a popular, gentle hike. This trail traces the route of the former Great Northern Railroads over Stevens Pass. Begin at Martin Creek, Scenic, or Wellington, off the Tye Road where you are. (No pass required at the Scenic trailhead.) If you start at the Martin Creek trailhead, about the first three miles are ADA accessible. Much of the trail also has interpretive markers.

3. Ohme Gardens

3327 Ohme Rd
Wenatchee, WA 98801
(509) 662-5785
www.ohmegardens.com
Fee to enter

The Ohme Gardens are the dream of Herman and Ruth Ohme, who in 1929 bought what was then a dry bluff with a gorgeous view of the Cascades and the Columbia River valley (and no industrial park, yet). They set out to create an oasis of green meadows, turquoise pools, and winding trails lined with flourishing evergreens.

Let's diverge here a moment to remind you of a promise I make in my Pam on the Map books: whatever I experience, I'll be honest about it.

I first heard about the Ohme Gardens a very long time ago; however, since they're quite a drive from Seattle, I'd never made it out there. With a research trip for Leavenworth planned, the time seemed right to drive the extra 20 miles to the Gardens and see what there was to see.

I'm not entirely sure why, but I was a little underwhelmed.

Maybe it was the fact that one edge of the gardens now looks down over a very industrial part of Wenatchee, which somewhat ruins the magic. Or maybe, living in the Pacific Northwest, spectacular landscapes are an everyday thing, and I've become too used to beauty? As they say, your mileage may vary. This isn't intended as a negative review, just an honest one.

Would I go again? I think I would go once, yes, if for no other reason than to support an effort to create and nurture wonderful natural spaces in our world. These gardens, largely built by hand on rocky, uneven, difficult terrain, were created as a labor of love. If you like gardens, go once. Then you can decide for yourself if it's worth going again.

But back to our road trip. If you decide to visit the gardens, when you hit Leavenworth just wave and keep going another 20 or so miles to Ohme Gardens. Park in the shady lot, pay your entrance fee, pick up a map of the gardens, and head on in. How long it takes you to go through the gardens depends on how many trails you intend to follow; I'd say an hour is a good estimate, though.

Note that while there are some parts of the gardens that are suitable for people of all walking abilities, much of it is steep, uneven, or narrow, and may feel a bit dangerous to those for whom balance and agility are a challenge. Wear good walking shoes for this stop.

Optional Side Trip:

Peshastin Pinnacles State Park: On your way back toward Leavenworth, check out Peshastin Pinnacles State Park. These sandstone spires poke out of the earth like the sharp teeth of an enormous monster long fossilized. Great for photographers, rock climbers, or general appreciation of the wonders of nature. The hikes tend to be on the steep side, but the 34-acre day-use park is also a nice spot for picnicking, bird watching, and relaxing in the great outdoors. 7201 N Dryden Rd, Cashmere, WA 98815, parks.state.wa.us/565/ Peshastin-Pinnacles.

4. Leavenworth

Map coordinates: 47.594234, -120.665354
www.leavenworth.org

Make your way back to US 2 and head west, back into Leavenworth. Find a parking space somewhere (I tend to park on the edges of town and walk in), and get ready to meander!

Leavenworth is one of a handful of cities in the U.S. that have some kind of Christmas celebration going on year-round. The problem with making a day trip out of Leavenworth is that there's so much to do, there's no way you can do it all in one day. This town is well worth staying a few nights. Nonetheless, if a day is all you have, it makes for a fantastic day trip (and one in which you can scope out ideas for future visits). Only a couple of hours away from Seattle geographically, it feels like another continent.

What's on in Leavenworth? Take your pick. This is not just a summer destination but a year-round draw. Check the town's website before you: a comprehensive, well-organized, and up-to-date calendar at their website makes it easy to find out what's going on. Classes, live music, historical walking tours, wine hikes, garden tours, farmers markets, theater productions, goings-on in the park, you name it, it's on the calendar. What else? Film festivals, Taste Leavenworth, Leavenworth Wine and Chocolate, BirdFest, Maifest, Annual Icicle Creek Chamber Music Festival, Leavenworth Ale Fest, International Accordion Festival, Bavarian Bike & Brew Festival, Wine Walk, Wenatchee River Salmon Festival, Washington State Autumn Leaf Festival, Oktoberfest, a Downtown Christmas Market, Christmas Lighting Festival, Bavarian Ice Festival, and more: Leavenworth has it all.

What's more, you can also quench your taste for just about every kind of outdoor activity as well. Horseback riding, standup paddleboarding, fishing and hunting, golfing, hiking and running, bicycling and mountain biking, birding, rafting and kayaking and tubing, zip lining, rock climbing … and then, of course, there are the winter activities, too, from dog sled rides to skiing to sledding and tubing and beyond. Oh, and, the shopping. Don't forget the shopping, and eating, and wine tasting!

A few ideas from which to pick and choose:

Short Hikes
Blackbird Island: A city park trail which saunters on the island on a 2-mile loop alongside the Wenatchee River.
Icicle Creek Interpretive Trail: A 1-mile loop; trailhead at the Leavenworth Fish Hatchery, two miles down Icicle Creek Road (12790 Fish Hatchery Rd, Leavenworth, WA 98826).
(There are tons of longer hikes in the area, too!)

Wineries and Wine Tasting
In downtown Leavenworth there are tons of Wine Tasting Rooms:
- Swakane Winery Tasting Room (725 Front Street)
- D'Vinery (617 4-A Front Street)
- Ryan Patrick Vineyards (636 Front Street, Suite 2)
- Kestral Vintners (843 Front Street, Suite B)
- Taste of Icicle Ridge Winery (821 Front St, Suite B)
- And more!

Nearby Wineries:
- Boudreaux Cellars (4551 Icicle Road, Leavenworth)
- Silvara Vineyards (77 Stage Road, Leavenworth)
- Wedge Mountain Winery (534 Saunders Road, Peshastin)
- Cascadia Winery (10090 Main St, Ste F, Peshastin)
- Icicle Ridge Winery (8977 North Road, Peshastin)
- Eagle Creek Winery (10037 Eagle Creek Road, Leavenworth)

Wineries can come and go, so check in advance to be sure the one you want to visit is still there.

Other Downtown Shops

The Cheesemonger's Shop
819 Front Street, Suite F (downstairs)
(509) 548-9011
www.cheesemongersshop.com
Specializes in meats and cheeses from around the world. Great for packing your picnic.

The Oil and Vinegar Cellar
633 Front St, Suite F (down the stairs)
(509) 470-7684
www.oilandvinegarcellar.com
Specially infused olive oils and aged balsamic vinegars. Full disclosure: the owner is the sister of the wife of my second cousin once removed (I think?). But we didn't know that when we first found the shop, and it's irrelevant when I take people there for the first time. Taste a few of these amazing balsamic vinegars and the vast

array and deliciousness will quickly entice you to take advantage of the special bulk pricing (ask at the counter).

Kris Kringl
907 Front Street
(509) 548-6867
www.kkringl.com
Step inside and be surrounded by Christmas, all year long. Christmas trees, ornaments, nutcrackers, and every manner of decoration await.

And, of course, there are plenty of shops with ice cream and other sweets, as well as restaurants serving delicious food. The sausages at the very popular Leavenworth Sausage Garden are savory and scrumptious, but if the line is too long, turn around and head across the street to the München Haus Bavarian Grill and Beer Garden, where the wursts are also fabulous and the condiment choices are endless.

More Activities

There's no shortage of outfitters looking to hook you up with the activities you most desire. Having not utilized them, I won't recommend any, but it's worth checking out. Several companies offer wine tours, including one that even offers a "Whitewater and Wine Tour."

If you plan to stay later in the evening, check the calendar for live music. Most nights you can find something somewhere in town!

5. Deception Falls

Map coordinates: 47.715099, -121.195836

You may decide by this point that your day has been long enough and you're tired and it's time to just head home. Well, let me tell you: I've saved the best for last. Depending on how long you want to stay, this can be literally a ten-minute stop, and it's beyond worth it.

Some of you may be thinking, "Deception Falls? Does she mean Deception Pass? And isn't that up north by Whidbey Island?" The answers to your questions are No, I don't; and Yes, that is where Deception Pass is. And you are not alone if you are confused. I have an iPhone, and when I type Deception Falls into the Maps app that comes with it, it insists time and again that I must mean either Deception Pass or Snoqualmie Falls. For whatever reason, Deception Falls, one of the most spectacular and most accessible falls in our area, has largely fallen under the radar.

So shhhh. I really shouldn't be telling you about this place. Let's just keep it between us, shall we?

Going west again on US 2, shortly after milepost 57, the turn-off to Deception Falls will be on your right. (Conversely, if you're skipping ahead and are stopping here on the way east, the turnoff is, as you might have guessed, shortly after milepost 56, on your left.) Park in the lot and head to the trail at the east end of the lot. From there, climb down a few very broad steps and walk the very short path to the bridge over these roaring falls. If you're there in early spring after heavy rains, the falls will nearly touch the underside of the bridge as the water rushes by. Cross the bridge and climb several wet and slippery stairs to get another view. The roar of the water is so loud up there you'll hardly be able to hear your companions—whether that's a good thing or not is for you to say.

If this quick view of the falls is not enough, you can also ramble along a nature trail with interpretive signage. It's about a half mile long, with a few spokes off the main loop that lead to viewing areas of the more breathtaking spots, including more magnificent falls. There is a spot toward the west end of the trail that can be a bit dicey, if they haven't fixed it; depending on how agile you are, it may be anything from fairly easy to impassible, and you might get your feet wet. You can, however, always turn around and go back the other way.

Once you've soaked in enough mist and awe, head back to US 2 and head home.

Day Trip Packing List

If you're going to be gone all day, you'll want to bring some essentials with you. Depending on where you're going, who you're going with, time of year, and how prepared you like to be, here's a very thorough checklist. Take what you need!

- Camera and tripod
- Phone
- Back-up batteries for camera (and anything else that needs a battery)
- Back-up battery chargers
- Phone car charger (plus that for the phones of any friends coming along)
- Water
- Cooler and ice
- Folding chairs
- Blankets
- Beach towels
- Flip flops or appropriate footwear

- Snack food
- Picnic lunch
- Sunglasses
- Bug spray
- Suntan lotion
- Chapstick
- First aid kit with bandaids, antibacterial cream, mole skin
- Medications you may need, headache medicines
- Extra clothes if you might get wet or dirty
- Rain clothes if it might rain
- Flashlight
- Maps
- Credit card / ATM card / cash
- Corkscrew
- Can opener
- Napkins, utensils, plates, cups
- Swiss army knife
- Hand wipes / baby wipes / hand sanitizer
- Hair elastics
- Day bag / backpack
- Plastic bags for garbage or wet clothes
- *Pam on the Map: Seattle Day Trips*

Pam on the Map: Seattle Day Trips, Book 2

Ideas and plans for *Seattle Day Trips: Book 2* are already underway! If you enjoyed this book and found it useful, be sure to sign up for my mailing list, so you won't miss out. You'll get very few emails (generally only when a new book is out), and your email address will never be sold or shared. www.pamstucky.com.

Photos and Reviews

Photos

I debated adding photos to these books, but in the end decided not to due to issues of cost and quality control. But fear not, photo-loving people! I've put a bunch of pictures up on my website. Just go to www.pamstucky.com/pamonthemap/seattle1 and peruse some Day Trip photos to your heart's content!

Reviews

Word-of-mouth and reader reviews are my best marketing. If you enjoyed this book, I would be so grateful if you would tell your friends and/or write a quick review! And be sure to find me online and say hello! Thank you!

Acknowledgments

Thank you to Pat at the Bellingham Visitor Center (he's there Friday mornings) for being such a delightful guy to talk with, and for giving ideas for the Fairhaven trip and suggesting the route for the Mount Baker / Artist Point trip.

My gratitude to @MountRainierNPS and @VisitRainier on Twitter, for helping me out with a few key points, including the fact that "Mount" is preferred over "Mt." when referring to the mountain.

I'm grateful, to friends and family who traveled along with me on my various trips, kept me company, and shared in the adventures, including Lisa Sivertson, Shannon Pitton, Dick Stucky and Beth Stucky.

Thank you to Dick Stucky and Beth Stucky for reading early drafts of the chapters and giving me the wisdom of their own experience. And, of course, for their eternal love, support, encouragement, and everything else under the sun.

More by Pam Stucky

The Balky Point Adventures (MG/YA sci-fi)

"Aliens, infinite universes, ghosts AND time travel ... a winning literary combination if ever there was one." — *Just One More Chapter reviews*

This smart and unforgettable middle grade / young adult science fiction adventure series takes teens Emma, Charlie, Eve, and Ben, along with brilliant but quirky Dr. Waldo and a host of others, on adventures through time and space. Inspired the timeless wonder and fantasy of *A Wrinkle in Time*, with just a dash of *Doctor Who*, the Balky Point Adventures are for readers of all ages who love a good romp through the imaginative marvels of the universes, delivered with heart and wonder. Exciting and imaginative, courageous and thought-provoking, this series commends the strength of compassion, and the inherent power within each person to change the world ... or the universe.

Includes: *The Universes Inside the Lighthouse*, *The Secret of the Dark Galaxy Stone*.

The Wishing Rock series (contemporary fiction)

"It was just what the doctor ordered, fresh, quirky, funny in places and seasoned with wisdom. Light without being frivolous." — *Tahlia Newland, author*

The Wishing Rock books take us to the fictional town of Wishing Rock, in which all the town's residents live in the same building. In this *Northern Exposure*-esque slice-of-life series, letters between the neighbors and their friends chronicle the twists and turns of the characters' daily lives, and are interspersed with recipes tried and tested by the characters themselves. These novels, filled with wit, wisdom, and recipes, offer up insightful exploration of the ideas of community, relationships, happiness, hope, forgiveness, risk, trust, and love.

Includes: *Letters from Wishing Rock*, *The Wishing Rock Theory of Life*, and *The Tides of Wishing Rock* (all novels with recipes); *From the Wishing Rock Kitchens: Recipes from the Series* completes the series, with a compilation of all the recipes in the first three books.

Death at Glacier Lake (mystery)

"This is a neat little mystery with the rare virtue that the setting and characters are as interesting as the unfolding story... A reflective tone, with heart and insight into human frailty and strength, made this a very worthwhile read." — *Amazon reader*

Pam's first mystery, written in a traditional "whodunit" style, has already captivated fans of this popular genre. For two decades, the lush, isolated forests of the North Cascades have hidden a secret. Now, twenty years later, a mysterious contest has brought Mindy Harris back to the area she thought she'd left behind forever. A seemingly innocent creative design firm shows up for a company retreat, but all goes awry when one of their own turns up dead. Was it an accident? Murder? And how does the unsolved mystery from twenty years ago play into it all?

The Pam on the Map series (travelogues)

"I couldn't resist reading the entire book, both for the wit and chuckles that I found on nearly every page, and to make sure I didn't miss any of the useful tips that were scattered throughout. I'm big on pre-trip research, and I found some tips in this book that I haven't seen elsewhere." — *Emily, Amazon reader*

In her Pam on the Map series, Pam sets out to discover and connect with people and places, and to take readers along on her adventures through her almost real-time reports. Raw and real, Pam's tales are infused with candid honesty, humorous observations, and perceptive insights. Pam's descriptive, entertaining, conversational style brings her trips alive, making readers feel as though they're traveling right along with her.

Though they're not guidebooks, the Pam on the Map books are still informative and illuminating, providing useful tips and plentiful ideas for people who might want to follow along in Pam's footsteps.

Includes: ***Pam on the Map: Iceland***, ***Pam on the Map: Seattle Day Trips***, ***Pam on the Map (Retrospective): Ireland***, and ***Pam on the Map (Retrospective): Switzerland***.